HABERMAS:
AN INTRODUCTION

Other Works in
The Pennbridge Introductory Series

Adorno   by Willem van Reijen
Foucault   by Hinrich Fink-Eitel

HABERMAS:
AN INTRODUCTION

Detlef Horster
with contributions by
Willem van Reijen

Translated from the German
by Heidi Thompson

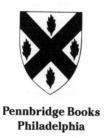

Pennbridge Books
Philadelphia

Pennbridge Books, March 1992
Translation copyright ©1992 by Pennbridge Communications Inc.

All rights reserved under International and Pan-American Copyright
Conventions. Published in the U.S. by Pennbridge Communications Inc.
Originally published in Germany as Habermas zur Einführung by Junius
Verlag GmbH (Hamburg).
Copyright 1988

Library of Congress Catalog Card Number
92-60244

Portions of the translation of *The Theory of Communicative Action* used in
this book were taken from the English translation by Thomas McCarthy
(Boston: Beacon Press, 1984).

Design and Typesetting: Falco & Falco Incorporated
Printing: Versapress

Manufactured in the United States
ISBN 1-880055-01-5

Dedicated to
my first philosophy teachers
Paul Kremer
and
Karl-Heinz Volkmann-Schleck

CONTENTS

Editor's Note: When a work has been translated into English,
the English title is used. Otherwise the title will appear in German,
French, etc.

The Publisher would like to thank Gordon Yee and James Buckwalter
for their assistance in the preparation of this volume.

PREFACE

This introductory volume presents the work of Jürgen Habermas from several different perspectives. The first chapter outlines the development of his thought leading to the *Theory of Communicative Action*. Here it will become clear that his social analysis does not confine itself to research, but rather proceeds logically to the sphere of politics, a challenge to which Habermas responds as a combative democrat.

The next two chapters systematically deal with two topics that are central to Habermas's linguistic and social philosophy. Chapter 2 treats the change in paradigm from ontology to philosophy of consciousness and linguistic philosophy. In this transition the influence of Husserl and Mead on Habermas's ideas becomes visible in the terms "lifeworld" and "intersubjectivity." Second, the historical distinction of reason in its three moments and Habermas's attempt at a reconstruction of their unity are treated. The two principal emphases of this introductory volume are central to Habermasian thought; from the discussion of these two main points, it should be possible for the reader independently to penetrate deeper into the works of Habermas, as well as relate more peripheral issues to the central concerns.

Following chapter 3, Willem van Reijen provides a comprehensive summary of the *Theory of Communicative Action*, with which Habermas completed his theoretical endeavors up to that point. Habermas's volume is very broad in scope, and the overview van Reijen provides is most useful to students and philosophical laity who want to inform themselves about the subjects treated here, and also to those who, for the time being, do not choose to tackle the oeuvre itself.

Very few passages have been taken from the first edition of this book (*Habermas: Eine Einführung*, 1980). At that point Habermas's major work and some of the preliminary works preceding it had not yet appeared, nor had his other contributions to the philosophical and political discussion of the 1980s. In this edition, which is actually a completely new book, an interview with Jürgen Habermas that provides a good insight into the development of his thought has been reprinted unchanged. This interview may be read first by readers for whom biographical information is a help to understanding theory.

1

JÜRGEN HABERMAS: SOCIAL ANALYST AND COMBATIVE DEMOCRAT

As early as ten years ago, Jürgen Habermas was described in *Der Spiegel* as the "most intellectually powerful" philosopher in the Federal Republic of Germany. Others confirmed that this discussion of his "enormous significance" for contemporary social sciences was a tremendous understatement, particularly because his influence is not limited to only one field. His work embraces the spheres of political theory, psychology, the theory of evolution, pedagogy, linguistic philosophy, and other fields as well.

In fact, it is impossible to reduce Jürgen Habermas's work over the past thirty years to one simple formula. Many who consciously experienced the beginnings of the student movement in the 1960s first encountered his name when they read his book on the structural transformation of the public sphere. I am sure I am not the only one for whom reading that work led to a change in my view of democracy in the Federal Republic. Why Habermas wrote this book probably can be understood best from his life history.

The year 1945 was decisive for Habermas's political and theoretical development. The first sixteen years of his life were spent in the provincial environment of Gummersbach, in North Rhine-Westphalia west of Cologne, during the rule of the Nazis. He was not aware of the extent of the Nazis' reign of terror. Through the documentary films that he saw after the war it became clear to him that the Allied victory was a liberation from a criminal tyranny. In the following years, he had great expectations for the model of democracy that the Americans and the British attempted to implant in the western sectors. Habermas experienced his first political disappointment with the formation of the new government in 1949. He had not believed it possible that a man like Hans Christian Seebohm, who indisputably embodied the continuity of National Socialist influence, would be able to sit as Transportation Minister in a Parliament that had committed itself to democracy. The fear that a real break with National Socialism had not occurred was confirmed in events such as this. As we know today, the reinstatement of judges, officials, doctors, and others who had followed Hitler and supported fascism cuts a broad path through the years of the German economy's reconstruction. This phenomenon must have been perceptible at the time. There had been no fundamental transition to democracy, or at least the majority of the population had not consciously completed such a transition.

However, according to Habermas in the interview printed in this volume, his generation had then learned "that the bourgeois constitutional state in its French or American or British form, is an historical achievement. An important biographical distinction exists between those who experienced what a half-hearted democratic republic like the Weimar Republic can lead to and those who became politically conscious later on."

In this statement, Habermas is referring to people who, both during the Weimar Republic and again in the post-war West German state, criticized the potential for development on the part of a state that used a bourgeois constitution as a mask of legitimation. But the contrast between National Socialism and the new state of affairs allowed Habermas's generation to hope that a real democracy could develop and become firmly established.

From 1949 on, Habermas studied philosophy. As early as 1954 he completed his philosophical dissertation on Schelling. A crucial experience for him was the appearance of Heidegger's *Introduction to Metaphysics*. Habermas comments, "I then saw that Heidegger, in whose philosophy I lived, gave and published this lecture in 1935 without a single word of explanation; that was what really upset me." Habermas made this statement in the interview mentioned above, and he added that he then realized that philosophy could not be separated from political intentions; otherwise, like Heideggerian philosophy, it would simply pass by contemporary events that affect human beings in their relationship to society and the environment. In the years to come, Habermas was to be inspired by Lukács' *History and Class Consciousness* and by Horkheimer and Adorno's *Dialectic of Enlightenment*, both of which raised social-philosophical questions. Given this knowledge, it is a great irony that, of all people, Adorno then refused to accept *Structural Transformation of the Public Sphere* from Habermas as a postdoctoral thesis.

It was precisely this work which attempted to elucidate the conditions in the Federal Republic through a social-philosophical way of thinking. In this work, Habermas analyzes the dark sides of the system whose advantages seemed so obvious to him. Still, he recognized early on that mistakes were built into this system and that they could lead to serious distortions. Beginning with his book he starts from the assumption that bourgeois society has ideals that it does not realize, and that these ideals at the same time function as legitimations that are necessary to maintain social order.

Habermas examines the term "public sphere" carefully because, in his opinion, it is an essential ingredient in the proof of a structural transformation in society. The basic purpose of the "public sphere" as an institution was to monitor and legitimate power via the medium of public discussions. This concept is constituted in the establishment of the bourgeois state under the rule of law—in the transition to organized capitalism. Habermas describes the decline of this institution as follows:

> Only this dialectic of a progressive societization of the state simultaneously with an increasing "stateification" of society gradually destroyed the basis of the bourgeois public sphere—the separation of state and society. Between the two and out of the two, as it were, a repoliticized social sphere emerged to which the distinction between "public" and "private" could not be usefully applied.[1]

During this process, the public sphere, in its liberal form, dissolves; today, a public sphere must be created or "made." It now only serves to mark an area where competition exists between different interest groups, and publicity is used to gain approval and prestige. The administrative authority increasingly becomes the public authority. The government's decisions are accepted with the justification that the matters at hand are governmental affairs and not for the public to comprehend or criticize. Moreover, criticism can be rejected with the charge of a lack of objectivity. The capacity of the press to create a discriminating public is limited by its dependence on advertising, as well as governmental control over press agencies.

The organization of the enlightened public into parties is ruled out to the extent that the parties become instruments of power for the purpose of serving their own bureaucrats. Powers are then given over to the public, and these powers themselves represent the interests of power or exert power. The public sphere came into being to check power and itself then became power, not least of all because human beings, conditioned by the rule of instrumental reason, lack the proper value orientations to exercise criticism over the public sphere.

Nevertheless, Habermas sees a solution: "the rationalization of the exercise of social and political authority."[2] From this point on, he links social analysis with the search for the possibility of rational domination, which the bourgeois public sphere can no longer achieve. The hope that is tied to it for the reinstatement of a regulating principle of reason led him to the very apt description as a late proponent of the Enlightenment. This term effectively exhibits the intent to which Habermas remains true throughout his theoretical efforts: he is concerned with exposing the conditions that affect the possibility of understanding, as this understanding has been given to the human race to find solutions to the conflicts that arise from actions. This purpose at the same time points to the central question of critical social theory as Habermas seeks to develop it by taking up both Marx and critical theory. How can the standard of criticism be identified if it cannot be the standard of "objective knowledge" as it exists in positivism?

Habermas's first attempts at the relation between theory and practice (*Theory and Practice*, 1963) furnish a critique of positivism and revolve above all around the question of how empirical-analytic science, as the productive force behind industrial development in its relation to the social lifeworld, "can be reflected and brought into the domain of rational debate."[3] In order to clarify the issue of the consequences of scientific and technological progress, Habermas introduces a distinction that remains fundamental for his work as a whole: the distinction between labor and communicative action. Habermas equates the term labor with purposive rational behavior. By this term he means

> either instrumental action or rational choice or a combination of both. Instrumental action addresses *technical rules* based on empirical knowledge... Behavior of rational choice addresses strategies based on analytical knowledge... Purposive rational action realizes specified goals under given conditions.[4]

Communicative action, on the other hand,

> addresses norms that are *necessarily valid*, that define reciprocal behavioral expectations and must be understood and recognized

by at least two subjects who interact with one another. Social norms are supported by sanctions. The reason for such norms is objectified in colloquial conversation . . . The learned rules of purposive rational action equip us with the discipline of *abilities*; internalized norms equip us with the discipline of *personality structures*. Skills enable us to solve problems; motivations allow us to conform to norms.[5]

With this distinction, Habermas can now classify social systems and subsystems according to the predominant type of action. The distinction between the socio-cultural environment, and the subsystems of purposive rational action that have been allowed into this environment, is fundamental. With this consideration, the problem of the practical consequences of technological progress becomes the central question pertaining to the influence of technologically advancing systems on the environment. environment.

Within this scenario, Habermas productively tackled Marxism. Habermas determined that the inherent limitation of the Marxist method was that it sought to be appropriate for the society that it analyzed, a society in which all social relations are aligned according to the requirements of production and distribution. Within this framework, human beings appear first and foremost as the subjects of objectifying and alienating processes, their intellectual achievements solely purposive rational, and as such, those which are tied in to capitalist production. Habermas sees very clearly that "modern societies gradually press all areas of life into molds of economic and administrative rationality and suppress forms of practical rationality."[6] However, he maintains that even in capitalism, human beings do not let themselves be reduced to factors of production. Opposing normative structures always develop. Without these revolutionary processes would not be at all explicable. With respect to the Marxist analysis, Habermas criticizes the "reduction of the self-generative act of the human species to labor,"[6] and with his distinction between communicative and purposive rational action, he is able to follow two chains of historical-philosophic development:

> The human race learns not only in the dimension of technically useful knowledge, decisive for the development of production capacity, but rather also in the dimension of moral-political intention, crucial for structures of interaction. The rules of communicative action probably develop in reaction to changes in the area of instrumental and strategic action, but in so doing, they follow *their own logic.*[8]

After that, the neo-Marxists' conception of totality was as unacceptable for Habermas as Marxist theory. From his work on Schelling during his studies, he had gained the conviction that the philosophy of identity did not offer any solution, since nothing is left if one cannot distinguish anything: all cows are black at night. With this step, a line was drawn between Habermas and the philosophy of hope of Bloch, whom Habermas described as a "Marxist Schelling," as well as the negative dialectic of Adorno. Tying in with Kant, Habermas arrived at a new and viable grounding of the normative. The Marxist critical analysis does not adequately deal with the area of moral-practical reason, as it simply made the capability of knowledge, conditioned by social relations and located in the realm of the physical world, the subject of their criticism. Nor did the bourgeois social sciences treat the subject satisfactorily; indeed, both approaches revert back far beyond Kant. If man were to think and act only and exclusively in a purposive rational manner, alienation would be global and emancipation would be hopeless. On the other hand, Habermas showed that moral-practical reason, however disguised or unconscious, is also present in late capitalist societies and is evident in the communicative actions of everyday life. Habermas's works revolved ever closer around this conception for almost two decades before he unified them in his *Theory of Communicative Action.*

At the end of the 1960s and beginning of the 1970s, Habermas clarified his approach in a critical appraisal of the major movements in sociology. His criticism of the claims to universality made by both the empirical-analytic and the historical-hermeneutic method (*Zur Logik der Sozialwissenschaften*, 1967) made clear that a social theory cannot succeed without an interpretive understanding. It must, however, tie hermeneutic interpretation to ideological criticism. Against the method of interpretive understanding, Habermas objected (in *Hermeneutik und Ideologiekritik*, 1971) that domination can always be effective in that which brings about unification. Understanding must be expanded around the introduction of a concept that would allow for excluding the possibility of a forced consensus.

From this position, Habermas took up the debate with systems theory, above all with the ideas of Niklas Luhmanns. It is beyond the scope of this introduction to outline the mutually reciprocating criticism. The incompatibility of both positions can certainly be traced back to the dehumanized view of man in systems theory. This theory views society as a soulless mechanism — a view that Habermas took as the central point in his criticism — and it views human beings as the operating parts of a machine. In this period the theoretical outlines of Habermas were categorized with the term "communicative competence," and they increasingly integrated the influence of Anglo-American linguistic philosophy and developmental psychology. To a great extent, Habermas's theories developed in the process of debate with competing models of theory formation in the social sciences. These theories reached a provisional conclusion in the *Theory of Communicative Action*.

According to Habermas, with his *Theory of Communicative Action*, he wants "to confront the issue of the normative foundations of critical social theory, which was not treated at all,"[9] and to show that the "concepts of truth, freedom and justice are constitutively involved in the structures of linguistic communication as quasi-transcendental fundamental norms that are closely tied to one another."[10] On the different level of theory formation in the social sciences, the correlation between empirical analysis and normative preconditions should be clear enough. In response to the reproach that it is sacrilegious to maintain that the ideas of practical reason are valid in the empirical social sciences, Habermas laid himself open to rigorous questioning as to where he expected to find the normative foundations of a critical social theory without sinking into metaphysics.

Habermas believes that these normative foundations are to be found in language. Habermas's turning to language is easy to understand if we begin with the thought that there is no objective knowledge, and that the interests of the scientist, in accordance with which he determines the objects of his research, feed on his lifeworld. According to Habermas, this lifeworld consists of "individual abilities, intuitive knowledge of how one deals with a given situation; and socially accepted practices, the intuitive knowledge that one can rely on in a given situation, not less than that of underlying beliefs of which one is conscious." Understanding among people is only possible within the context of a familiar background; this knowledge of the environment is contained in language. Thus, the social scientist himself introduces into the communicational and scientific process a great number of unanalyzed preconditions. These underlying beliefs contained within language must also be included in the discussion; these normative foundations of a critical social theory can be analyzed via language. Here Habermas takes up Wittgenstein and the lifeworld theory of Husserl: "The social sphere of a shared lifeworld, which manifests itself in conversation, provides the key to the communication-theoretical concept of society."[12]

If we follow Habermas's analysis of cognizant interests, we must admit that objective knowledge is unable to escape being tied to the lifeworld. Individual abilities, intuitive knowledge, socially accepted practices and underlying beliefs—which may also be called prejudices (although not necessarily in the purely negative sense of the word)—shape our knowledge. In this respect, theoretical knowledge is always a moral-practical issue. This conclusion is also valid for the context of social analysis and political

action: "Only knowledge of structurally anchored but contrary
developmental tendencies widen our vision of opportunities for
practical intervention."[13] And a meaningful orientation in politics can only develop out of ethical or moral motives. Similarly,
Kant thought that politics could do nothing without first having
embraced morals; that is, without openly subscribing to some concept of good that lends meaning to political action. Aristotle con-
cluded his Nicomachean Ethics with this comment on its extension into the field of political science: "So that philosophy pertaining to human things can be brought to its conclusion according to the measure of our powers."

In this sense, unlike most scientists and philosophers, Habermas acted in a way consistent with his theories. Many times when
anti-democratic tendencies in our society emerged, Habermas,
as a combative democrat, spoke out. In the following, I would
like to provide two examples of this, as well as outline his position with respect to the "brashly accepted helplessness" of the
ex-left and post-left theories of the 1980s.

More than ten years ago, following the kidnapping and murd-
er of the President of the Employers' Federation, Hans Martin
Schleyer, a social climate allowing the hounding of radicals spread
[throughout the Federal Republic]; this period was later dubbed
the "German Autumn." Amid the flood of public indignation, reac-
tionary tendencies in legislation—and above all in political opinions expressed in public—found a more positive reception by the
people. At the time, Habermas reacted quickly, and in a letter
to Kurt Sontheimer dated September 19, 1977, he wrote:

> In their attempt to reactivate the conservative body of thought,
> those who formulate ideologies and their intellectual accomplices
> clearly find themselves in a difficult situation. The Nazis destroyed
> these traditions so thoroughly, that an "authentic conservatism"
> could no longer exist in the Federal Republic. . . Instead, the first
> two and one half post-war decades were a period in which, for
> the first time in Germany, the tradition of the Enlightenment—as
> maimed and uninterruptedly repressed as it has been—was shown

to its advantage in all its breadth from Lessing to Marx. It was made into the medium of intellectual productivity and was the missing link of political self-understanding. One moment of revolt on the part of the youth was then enough to usher in years of political conservatism. This reaction apparently now believes the time has come to kill two birds with one stone: to wash conservatism clean from the stigma of its association with bureaucratic terror, and to drive radical enlightenment into moral discredit through a denunciatory connection with the terrorism of the Red Army Faction.[14]

Habermas knows of only one means that is well established and, in his view, effective—exclusively in a political way—against the alienation of human beings brought on by society, and the support of this phenomenon by the right: Habermas stated, "We will fight for the beliefs of Enlightenment in our country."[15]

In a totally different context, Habermas reacted in a way that demonstrated sensitivity to the abandonment of the ideas of the Enlightenment. In the recent French philosophy following structuralism and Sartre, he discovered anti-rational tendencies which, stimulated by Nietzsche and Heidegger, could encourage neoconservative ideas. In the philosophical discussion in Germany, avowedly conservative theoreticians had become vocal and received a following—particularly since the climate of the political "turn" accommodated them. Once more, Habermas attacked the inadequate distinction between reason and understanding and the one-sided reduction of rationality to purposive rationality. In a series of individual critiques that were collectively published in 1985 in the book *The Philosophical Discourse of Modernity*, he addressed this issue. There he wrote:

The Party of neo-Conservatives stemming from right Hegelianism yields uncritically to the rampaging dynamism of social modernity, inasmuch as it trivializes reason back into understanding and rationality back into purposive rationality. Aside from a scientistically independent science, cultural modernity loses any normative character for it. The party of Young Conservatives stemming from Nietzsche outdoes the dialectical critique of the age—

inasmuch as it radicalizes the modern consciousness of time and unmasks reason as absolute purposive rationality—as a form of depersonalized exercise of power.[16]

Habermas had already criticized this narrowed conception of reason several times, among others with Max Weber. He now raised the point that with such a world view, the possibility of an alternative political practice is lost; moreover, this is a point which he already sees addressed by his teachers Horkheimer and Adorno.

The *Dialectic of Enlightenment* does not do justice to the rational content of cultural modernity that was captured in bourgeois ideals (and also instrumentalized along with them). I am thinking here of the specific theoretical dynamic that continually pushes the sciences, and even the self-reflection of the sciences, *beyond* merely engendering technically useful knowledge; I am referring, further, to the universalistic foundations of law and morality that have also been incorporated (in however distorted and incomplete a fashion) into the institutions of constitutional government, into the forms of democratic will formation, and into individualist patterns of identity formation; I have in mind, finally, the productivity and explosive power of basic aesthetic experiences that a subjectivity liberated from the imperatives of purposive activity and from conventions of quotidian perception gains from its own decentering.[17]

For Habermas, with all critical evaluation of the modern age, there are also aspects that can — and must — join with an alternative political practice if the ideas of liberty and justice are not to be relinquished to the right without a struggle. In a speech Habermas gave to the Spanish legislature on the invitation of the President of the Spanish Parliament, he emphasizes that modern society must find its orientations within itself,[18] in which case society's views will decide if alternative courses of action may be realized. In response to resignation and the argument that the potential for utopia is exhausted through the destructive development of the forces of production, as well as in response to neoconservative theories, he summarizes:

> It is by no means merely realism when a brashly accepted help-
> lessness increasingly takes the place of attempts at orientation
> directed towards the future. Viewed objectively, the situation may
> be confused. In this case, confusion is a function of the readiness
> to act of which a society believes itself capable. It is a matter of
> the confidence Western culture has in itself.[19]

Furthermore, Habermas believes in the ability of people to create self-organized protest against domination by economic and institutional power structures. But the change in paradigm from a society oriented toward labor to a society oriented toward communication changes the way in which the utopian traditions are taken up. An accurate social analysis in this scenario of all-structuring communication opens new utopian perspectives which replace the utopias of the laboring class that have already yielded to resignation. In conjunction with this development, Habermas sees the opening of the following perspective:

> Those conditions which distinguish themselves as normative are
> the necessary, but general, conditions for a communicative lifestyle
> and for a discursive method of developing an informed opinion.
> For those involved, this method could put them in the situation
> themselves to realize the concrete possibilities for a better and
> more secure life according to their own needs and insights from
> their own initiative.[20]

Two years after the appearance of the volume *Die neue Unübersichtlichkeit*, the new political events gave Habermas the opportunity to publish another volume of political statements. The book in question is *Eine Art Schadensabwicklung*, which appeared in 1987. In this work, Habermas gathers a series of political essays, speeches and interviews pertaining to different occasions from the two years prior to publication of the work. In this collection, his opinions on the so-called historians' dispute are emphasized. The historians, who were attempting to scientifically substantiate the ideology of a "turn," intended to offer Germans in the Federal Republic a national identity. If this identity is to be one of historical development, the period of fascism constitutes a great nuisance. Habermas calls this desire for a new identity "a kind of indemnification." This means nothing more than that it is an attempt to offer the individual, who constitutes a "social molecule" in the objectified industrial society and experiences an unavoidable alienation, a sense of meaning he can use to shape an identity, as a kind of recompense, so to speak. This attempt is also conspicuous in recent years with the many centenary celebrations of German cities, institutions, and great German statesmen: all Germans are not only the descendants of Adenauer, but naturally also of Bismarck and Frederick the Great.

The historians with whom Habermas has his dispute have all kinds of ideas about how to reduce National Socialism to an accident or de-emphasize it. For the theory that German culture and society attains higher levels than others (Michael Stürmer), the historical fact of National Socialism is a great nuisance. The interpretation that the Germans fell victim to a despotic regime or the persuasive charms of a demonic Adolf Hitler is comparatively mild. The remarks of Ernst Nolte weigh much more heavily, however. Habermas says of him, he is anything but a "fussing conservative narrator."[21] One asks himself, how can it occur to anybody to reduce the gas chambers of Auschwitz to "the technical process of gassing?" According to Nolte, it is only this emphasis on the technical process that distinguishes Auschwitz from the cruelties of the Russian Civil War, which, moreover, was the original of such phenomena; Auschwitz followed only later. Habermas's response: "The crimes perpetrated by the Nazis lose their singularity through the fact that they, as an answer to the Bolshevist threat of annihilation (which continues today) are at least made comprehensible. Auschwitz is reduced to the format of a technical innovation and explains itself with the fear of the 'Asian' threat by an enemy who still stands before our gates."[22] In this scenario, Hitler is defended, and if necessary, other things could be defended, as well.

I believe that we are not aware enough of what may once again be said and written in Germany, and what kind of atmosphere is created by this state of affairs. Habermas writes:

> We are still left with the simple fact that future generations grow up in a way of life in which *that* was possible. Our own life is bound to the life context in which Auschwitz was possible, perhaps not through contingent circumstances, but rather internally. Our way of life is tied to that of our parents and grandparents through a tapestry of familial, local, political and intellectual traditions that is difficult to penetrate. Thus, we are part of a historical milieu that has made us what and who we are today. None of us can steal away from this milieu because our identity, as individuals and as Germans, is inextricably interwoven within it.[23]

We must also stand by *this* tradition. It, too, belongs to our national identity. And we must deal with it if we do not want to be ideologically hypocritical or illogically dumb.

CHAPTER

2

HABERMAS'S
PHILOSOPHY OF LANGUAGE

LIFEWORLD AND INTERACTION

Philosophical enlightenment commences with doubt about naively handed down opinions that dominate in the realms of thought and perception. Habermas belongs to this tradition of enlightenment which began in ancient Greece with the skepticism of the Sophists. They asked if objective knowledge was possible at all, and if man did not bring an infinite number of assumptions into the process of knowledge. The question of whether or not objective knowledge is possible was pursued further in late antiquity and at the beginning of the Middle Ages by Plotinus and St. Augustine. They are more intensively occupied with the critical investigation of that with which one perceives, human thought, and less with the one which *is to be* perceived, the true nature of an entity. We are dealing here with the historical-philosophic change in paradigm from ontology—as the philosophy of Plato and Aristotle is called — to the philosophy of consciousness. "Ontological philosophy becomes impossible when any doubt exists that recognition of a true nature can succeed."[1]

At the beginning of the modern age, Descartes reaches the basic principles of his philosophy through radical doubt of naive trust in objectivity. He raises the question of by what right any claim to objective validity of judgement could be made, both in the sciences as well as in everyday life. This is the same question that motivated Habermas's research as well.[2] About 150 years after Descartes, Immanuel Kant demonstrates the boundaries of human knowledge, beginning with the different types of judgement; he calls it critique of reason. He teaches that we are able to know only that which we put into the world. We will never know, however, if the order that we thus give to the world is also the natural order of the world, and if things as we know them are, indeed, the things as they are by their nature. In making this distinction, Kant shows the conditions that shape the possibility of the objects that we recognize, and thus, the forms in which we think.

In *Critique of Pure Reason*, Kant exposed the possibility of our cognitive capacity. He did not, however, analyze the conditions determining the possibility of cognition. Husserl touches on this, as he asks about the foundations of conceptual thought, and finds them in "the surrounding world in which all of us (even I who am now philosophizing) consciously have our existence; here are also the sciences, as cultural facts in this world, with their scientists and theories."[3] In his book from 1968, *Knowledge and Human Interests*, Habermas follows Husserl:

> The research process organizes its object domain so that it corresponds to the interests that arise from the life process of the acting, and thus, knowing and exploring individual.... For this reason, technical and practical knowledge interests are not forces that steer cognition and should be turned off for the sake of objective knowledge; rather, to a much greater extent, they determine the aspect by which reality is objectivated, above all so that experience can be made accessible. The expression "interest" certainly is intended to indicate the unity of the life context in which cognition is embedded.[4]

Husserl maintains that people cannot simply "lose their interests and attitudes through a change; for each individual this would mean to cease to exist."[5]

According to Habermas, these views are contained in the "lifeworld," a term of Husserl that he takes up and defines as follows: the lifeworld "consists of individual skills, the intuitive knowledge of *how* one deals with a situation; and from socially acquired practices, the intuitive knowledge of what one can rely on in a situation, not less than, in a trivial sense, the underlying convictions."[6]

Human beings' communication with one another is only possible in the trusted surroundings of the lifeworld; moreover, knowledge of the lifeworld is contained in language. Thus, in the process of communication, we have at our disposal a comprehensive surrounding for our lifeworld. With the increasing rationalization of the lifeworld, the underlying convictions contained in language can be brought to discussion and made the object of scientific examination. Wittgenstein, who chooses language as a starting point for his analysis of human knowledge and its logic, points this out. Similar to Kant in his radicalness, Wittgenstein asks if we could even have sensual perceptions without language. The primacy of language only becomes the subject of philosophy in this context. In keeping with Wittgenstein's recognition of the fact that the boundaries of one's language are the boundaries of one's world, for Wittgenstein there is no logic preceding language.

Wittgenstein sees that the primacy of language becomes evident in its social use. This suggests to him that the logic of language might be traced back to the social aspect. Furthermore, according to Habermas, "the social space of a commonly inhabited lifeworld that opens up in a conversation provides the key to the communication-theoretical concept of society."[7] Here Habermas ties on to a philosopher who is eminently important for his theoretical development, and whom Habermas describes as "in fact, fundamental for my whole approach"[8]: George Herbert Mead. It was Mead who provided the impetus for a further thinking through of the issue of intersubjectivity, which was not resolved by Husserl.

Husserl maintains that views, intellectual spectrum and interest as the basis for perception of the world are located solely within the individual. However, the individual is not the sole possessor of his thoughts and actions. He is a socialized being, and a common frame of meaning is necessary for the perception of the world and intersubjective communication. Husserl experienced the greatest difficulties in progressing from the individual "I" to intersubjectivity: "Only by starting from the ego and the system of its transcendental functions and accomplishments can we methodically exhibit transcendental intersubjectivity and its transcendental communalization, through which, in the functioning system of ego-poles, the 'world for all,' and for each subject as world for all, is constituted."[9]

Looking at Mead's theory of symbolically communicated interactionism, we find the following argument: in keeping with the socialized world where interaction takes place largely in the form of gestures, a whole new social structure asserts itself in the form of symbolically communicated interaction. This new social structure presupposes the equality of all participants. Therefore, the symbols must have the same meaning for all participants in the interaction. This is the point at which linguistic symbols emerge. Social structures then develop through language because language contains that which is necessary to form the structure of a society and, correspondingly, to allow the functioning interaction of the members of the society: customs, cultural traditions, self-evident moral principles, technical skills.

Thus, according to Mead, language is the medium that draws all participants in the interaction into the communication community: it socializes the individual, and at the same time, obliges the members to become individuals. Habermas explains this idea as follows:

> The spatial and temporal individualization of the human race into individual specimens is not fundamentally regulated by means of

some genetic tendency that affects an individual organism regardless of its nature. Rather, subjects with the capacity to speak and act are constituted as individuals solely due to the fact that they grow into a particular language community in an intersubjectively divided lifeworld. In communicative educational processes, the identity of both the individual and the collective forms and preserves itself *simultaneously*. Specifically, the system of personal pronouns provides an unrelenting compulsion toward individualization that is built into communicatively oriented language use; through the same medium of everyday speech, socializing intersubjectivity appears simultaneously.[10]

because it is precisely that medium through which interaction becomes possible.

As Mead explains, this dual process that on the one hand individualizes but on the other hand socializes, emerges in communication:

In the process of communication, the individual is another before he becomes himself. By addressing himself in the role of another, he experiences himself as self. The development of organized group activities in human society—and the development of the organized game out of simple play in the experience of a child—provided the individual with a variety of different roles inasmuch as they were parts of social action and precisely out of the organization of these roles into a collective action the characteristic common to all of them appeared: they showed the individual what he had to do. The individual can now take a position for himself as "generalized other" in the attitude of the group or community. With this ability, the individual has become a definitive "self" relative to the social whole to which it belongs.[11]

Habermas kept to the challenge put forth by Husserl, which was to record the lifeworld systematically. Husserl had proposed this as the program of a new science (but he was never able to realize it). He wrote, "In opposition to all previously designed objective sciences, which are sciences on the ground of the world, this would be a science of the universal how of the pregivenness of the world, i.e., of what makes it a universal ground for any sort of objectivity. And included in this is the creation of a science of the ultimate grounds (*Gründe*) which supply the true force of all objective grounding, the force arising from its ultimate bestowal of meaning."[12] Habermas attempted to realize this traditional metaphysical program of Husserl by means of "universal pragmatics."

UNIVERSAL PRAGMATICS

The general theory of pragmatics has to do . . . with the reconstruction of the system of rules that lies at the bottom of the capacity of a subject to speak sentences in any situation whatsoever. At the same time, universal pragmatics requires that the ability of mature speakers to reconstruct, and thus, to lay sentences in reference to reality, so that they can take over the general pragmatic functions of description, expression and notification.[13]

The general and universal conditions for communicative action are sought here. In this search it is assumed that the standard conditions in every possible speech situation reoccur as general components. The starting point of the investigation begins with the most elementary unit of communicative action, namely the speech act.

J.L. Austin is really the one who ties on to the late work of Wittgenstein, and in so doing, takes the definitive step to an analysis of speech actions and overcomes semantic abstraction. He resolutely replaces the semantics of truth with a usable theory of meaning and the analysis of sentences by means of an analysis of the use of sentences in engagements. In the process, he gains leeway for dispelling the powers of illusion from the basic example: the declarative sentence. Austin begins to detach himself from an ontology that is tailored to the objective world as a totality of existing facts and has as a consequence the assertoric sentence as well as the propositional truth. With his concept of the illocutionary act, he opens the whole spectrum of speech to linguistic analysis. Wittgenstein's thesis that meaning was no longer to be sought in the relations of sentences to something in the world, but rather in the conventionally controlled use of these sentences has directed the attention of linguistic analysts to the richness of those linguistic games that "grammatically" regulate the employment of sentences in the context of life forms.[14]

Beginning with the elementary unit of language, the speech act, Habermas wants to attempt a systematic registration of that which constitutes a lifeworld.

First, I will show how Habermas came to the speech act through a series of abstract steps. These steps can be taken from the accompanying chart without further explanation.[15]

Of all the types of social action, Habermas is only interested in communicative action that is propositionally differentiated and linguistic. A statement, then, is propositionally differentiated if the propositional component of the statement can be separated from the illocutionary component without losing its meaning; that is, it must be invariant in the face of changing illocutionary potential, not least of all due to the different logic with which we perceive the object of our experience. If, for example, the propositional component of the sentence is my coming tomorrow, then this propositional component can be coupled with different illocutionary acts: as a notification (I notify you that I am coming tomorrow) or as a warning (I warn you that I am coming tomorrow). In both cases, the propositional component remains invariant. It has "as many applications as necessary depending on the context."[16]

The double structure of the speech act, allowing for the uncoupling of the illocutionary content from the propositional content of the speech act provides the conditions for this distinction. On the other hand, the greeting "Hello" is an example of a speech act that was not differentiated because the propositional content here exists and is based on convention, to be sure, but it is not expressed. The sign language of the traffic cop on the corner, for example, is propositionally differentiated and non-linguistic.

Institutional independence as a further abstract step is neces-

Instrumental Actions

Social Actions

Strategic Actions

Symbolic Actions

Communicative Actions

Propositionally Differentiated

Not Propositionally Differentiated

Linguistic

Non-Linguistic

Linguistic

Non-Linguistic

(Illocutionarily Shortened Speech Acts)

Institutionally Independent

Institutionally Dependent

Explicit

Implicit

Contextually Independent

Contextually Dependent

Analytic Unit

sary because with institutionally dependent speech acts, the norms assert themselves by means of institutional power. An example: "I hereby baptize you with the name Michael." This statement is valid because it is anchored in church law by means of a certain regulation. Instead of institutionally dependent norms, universally valid norms that are transmitted via the consciousness of every individual are sought, or norms that are internalized.

Speech actions must be explicit and not understandable only from the context. Explicit means that one has not only the speech act "I will come tomorrow" for analysis because without knowing the behavioral context, it would be difficult to recognize this statement as a promise, for example. That would require the speech act "I promise you that I will come tomorrow." The two requirements for explicit and contextually independent acts of speech are evident when one remembers that we are looking for general premises, not concrete ones for a certain single speech act.

From these abstractions Habermas obtains the standard form of speech actions that he puts at the foundation of his analysis.

The speech action that corresponds with all these abstraction prerequisites is composed of an illocutionary and a propositional component. Thus, it typically has a double structure: "The dominating sentence is used in a statement to communicate about objects."[17] We can again use the example "I promise you that I will come tomorrow." "I promise you" is the dominating or illocutionary component upon which my coming tomorrow depends. Here the illocutionary act in the speech action establishes the intention of the propositional content.[18] The propositional content has the meaning of the predicative understanding of the world, whereas the illocutionary act serves to establish an interpersonal relation.[19] Therefore, the illocutionary component is the one that causes a sentence to become an engagement: the transformation of sentences to engagements occurs in speech acts.

The aspect concerning the establishment of an interpersonal relation is central to a theory of communicative action[20] because it has to do with recognition of the normative structures of the society reflected within it. Because of this it must be asked where consists the illocutionary force of a statement? Habermas gives this definition: "The illocutionary force of an acceptable speech act consists . . . in its capacity to move the listener to depend on the speech-act-typical obligations of the speaker."[21] The illocutionary part of the sentence is the decisive moment of a speech act that, on the one hand, creates the speaker/listener relation and establishes the intention of the content; and on the other hand represents an offer on the part of the speaker that is tied to validity claims. "In the latter instance the speaker and listener can reciprocally engage one another because the speech-act-typical obligations are tied to cognitively testable validity claims."[22]

A term that is in need of explanation has been introduced here. What, then, are validity claims?

Habermas divides speech acts into four classes: communicative, constative, representative and regulative.

> The first class of speech acts, which I want to call *communicative*, serves to express different aspects of the very purpose of speech. It explicates the meaning of engagements via engagements. Each instance of speech presupposes an actual preconception of what it means to communicate in a language, to understand and misunderstand the engagements, to bring about a consensus, to dissent: in general, to know how to deal with language.

> Examples: say, express, speak, talk, ask, answer, respond, reply, agree, contradict, object, admit, mention, repeat, quote, etc.

> The second class of speech acts, which I want to call *constative*, serves to express the purpose of the cognitive use of sentences. It explicates the meaning of engagements through engagements. In the prototypical word for the assertoric mode, in "assert" two instances are united that appear separately in the two subclasses of these speech acts. On the one hand, "assert" belongs to the following group of examples: describe, report, inform, tell, elucidate, remark, set forth, explain, predict, etc. These examples stand for the assertoric use of engagements. On the other hand, "assert" belongs to the following group of examples: assure, protest,

affirm, deny, dispute, doubt. These examples elucidate the pragmatic purpose, especially of the truth claim of engagements.

The third class of speech acts, which I want to call *representative* (expressive) serves to express the pragmatic purpose of the self-portrayal of a speaker before an audience. It explicates the purpose of the speaker's engagement of intentions, views and experiences. The dependent clauses of propositional content are intentional clauses with verbs like know, think, mean, hope, fear, love, hate, like, wish, want, decide, etc. Examples are: expose, reveal, divulge, admit, express, conceal, veil, pretend, obscure, hide, keep secret, deny. (These speech acts appear in negated form: "I am not hiding from you that . . .")

The fourth class of speech acts, which I want to call *regulative*, serves to express the normative purpose of the established interpersonal relation. It explicates the meaning of the relation that the speaker/listener has with respect to behavioral norms. Examples are: command, ask, request, demand, warn, forbid, allow, suggest, refuse, oppose, obligate oneself, promise, agree, accept responsibility, confirm, support, vouch for, terminate, excuse, pardon, suggest, reject, recommend, assume, advise, warn, encourage, etc.[23]

Habermas then elucidates further: the communicative class of speech acts contributes to the comprehensibility of speech. In addition:

The employment of constative speech acts makes possible the distinction between a public world of intersubjectively recognized opinions and a private world of mere opinions (reality and appearance). The employment of representative speech acts makes possible the distinction between the individualized nature of which the subjects, capable of speaking and acting, mutually claim recognition; and the linguistic engagement, expressions and actions in which the subject appears (nature and manifestation thereof). The employment of regulative speech acts makes possible the distinction between empirical regularities that may be observed, and the prevailing rules that may be followed or broken (what is and what should be).[24]

If we look more closely now, we can make out different validity claims. Habermas speaks of the comprehensibility validity claim contained in communicative speech acts. The truth validity claim is contained in constative speech acts and the validity claim to rightness or appropriateness in the regulative speech acts. The validity claim of truthfulness is contained in the representative speech act. Thus, we have four validity claims, which Habermas later reduces to three, since the validity claim of comprehensibility is, in this sense, not a validity claim, but rather a rule of understanding.

The illocutionary component of speech action on the one hand creates the speaker/listener relation and establishes the purpose of the propositional component; on the other hand, certain validity claims are raised along with this component. They are presupposed as not problematic in each instance of speech. If the validity claims become problematic, the discourse protects the conditions of communicative action, in which only the truth and rightness or appropriateness claims can be realized discursively.[25] If the listener doubts the truth claim, this doubt certainly may be assuaged even within colloquial communication if the speaker supports his engagement with a further engagement. After this, communicative action may be continued. Let's assume that the speaker says, "My mother is coming tomorrow." If the listener doubts this with the question—"How do you know?"—the speaker can support the veracity of his statement with another engagement: "She just called." Now that the truth claim has been protected, the communication can be continued with the question, "What does she want here?" The answer is: "She wants to visit her aunt in the hospital."

> If the *comprehensibility* of an engagement is problematic, we ask questions of the following nature: How do you mean that? How am I to take that? What does that mean? We call answers to such questions *interpretations*. If the *truth* of the propositional content of an engagement is problematic, we ask questions of the following nature: Is it really like you say? Why is it so and not different?

We meet these questions with *claims* and *explanations*. If the right-ness or appropriateness of the norm that lies at the bottom of the speech act is problematic, we ask questions like: Why did you do that? Why didn't you behave differently? Are you allowed to do that? Shouldn't you behave differently? We answer these questions with *justifications*. In an interactional context, if we doubt the *truthfulness* of an opposite number, then we ask questions like: Is he deceiving me? Is he deceiving himself?[26]

DISCOURSE THEORY

If no consensus is reached in understanding-oriented speech, a transition to the level of discourse is necessary. In discourse, the validity of the validity claims made implicitly in communicative action can be discussed explicitly.

Habermas comments on the two forms of communication as follows:

Under the heading "action" I introduce that area of communication in which we silently presuppose and recognize implied validity claims in engagements (even in assertions) in order to exchange information (that is, behavior-related experiences). Under the heading "discourse" I introduced the form of communication characterized by argumentation in which validity claims that have become problematic are made the subject of discussion and examined relative to their legitimacy. In order to entertain a discourse, we must in a way step out of behavioral and experiential contexts; here we exchange not information, but rather arguments that serve to establish (or reject) problematic validity claims.[27]

Not all validity claims may be examined in discourse. Comprehensibility is the requirement for all successful communication. Moreover, one cannot discursively examine the doubt of whether a speaker means what he says, or whether the truthfulness claim is met. The truthfulness of an engagement (for example, if someone will really keep a promise he makes) can only be examined when one asks if the speaker is consistent and translates his promise into action, and if he continues to act consistently and follows the rule that he accepts. For example, a speaker behaves truthfully if he himself follows the recommendation he makes to his listener. Then one can eliminate the conclusion that the intentions he expresses do not coincide with those he verbally supports. Thus, on this level we may find the claim to reciprocal reliability, without which a speech act could not be fulfilled completely. We must return to contexts of action for the vindication of truthfulness claims, so the truthfulness validity claim can not be put into discourse because discourse is relieved of the burden of action.

The validity claims of rightness and truth, on the other hand, can be put into discourse. In theoretical discourse, assertions and explanations are transformed; the same holds true in practical discourse for justifications. "The discursive grounds change assertions to propositions, explanations to theoretical explanations, justifications to theoretical justifications."[28] Here the connecting link between theory and practice appears in the form of a flexible transition from communicative action to discourse, a concretization of this connection and in no way a polarization, as Tuschling asserts.[29]

But now before the logic of theoretical discourse can be discussed in detail, we must still address the question of who the participants in the discourse may be.

Habermas first suggests the sensibleness of a potential discourse participant as a criterion. However, to distinguish a true from a false consensus, we would have to know how we may determine the sensibleness of the participants in the discourse. Habermas believes it makes sense "to measure the sensibleness of a speaker by the *truthfulness of his engagements*. The engagements of a speaker are truthful if he deceives neither himself nor others. . . . In order to determine the *truthfulness of engagements, we then return to the rightness or appropriateness of actions.*"[30] Examining the appropriateness of actions requires an examiner who is competent in the rules. In order to determine this in both cases, that is, in order to avoid that the one being examined and the examiner himself conspire to fix competence in the rules, both must enter into a discourse. "We cannot judge the appropriateness in an action externally; we must make sure of it as participants of an interaction; or if the consensus that has been worked out should fail, we must attempt to reach a discursive understanding among the participants themselves."[31] That leads us back again to our initial consideration:

> When in doubt, the distinction between a true and a false consensus must be determined through discourse. But the result of the discourse again depends upon the attainment of a durable consensus. The consensus theory of truth makes us aware that no decision can be made about the truth of statements without reference to the competence of possible judges, and moreover, no decision can be made about this competence without evaluating the truthfulness of their engagements and the appropriateness of their actions. The idea of the true consensus demands from the participants in the discourse the ability to distinguish reliably between appearance and reality, nature and manifestation, what is and what should be in order to competently judge the truth of statements, the truthfulness of engagements and the rightness or appropriateness of actions.[32]

There is, however, no criterion that is independent of discourse. For this reason, if we can find the prerequisites for a discourse only in the discourse itself, then we go around in circles as much in the search for evaluation criteria on the sensibleness of discourse participants as in determining expert knowledge of the rules. If this is true, then it is a wonder that conversations are still held, that everyday conversations arise, and that we recognize our conversation partner. And furthermore, each participant in the conversation trusts himself to be able to distinguish a true consensus from a false one. This phenomenon requires an explanation. For this, Habermas introduces the concept of the "ideal speech situation."

Habermas explains this phenomenon as follows: in every discourse we "mutually *assume* an ideal speech situation. The ideal speech situation is characterized such that each consensus that can be achieved under its conditions is valid as a true consensus per se. *The anticipation of the ideal speech situation* is a guarantee that we may associate *the claim to a true consensus with a consensus that has actually been attained.*"[33] Only if we make reference to the ideal speech situation in every discourse, do "the individual informal constraints of the better argument"[34] dominate in discourse.

For the ideal speech situation, and along with it, for the achievement of a discourse, Habermas gives four conditions derived from the four classes of speech acts named:

1. All potential participants to a discourse must have the same chance to employ communicative speech acts so that at all times they may open discourse, as well as perpetuate it through address and reply, question and answer.

2. All participants in a discourse must have the same chance to put forward interpretations, assertions, recommendations, explanations and justifications, and to problematize their validity claim, to establish or reject it, so that no preconceived opinion escapes discussion or criticism for any length of time...

3. The discourse allows only for speakers who have an even chance as active subjects to employ representative speech acts, that is, those who can express their views, feelings and wishes... (This is the guarantee) that the active subjects are true to themselves, also as when they function as participants in the discourse, and they make their internal nature transparent.

4. The discourse allows only for speakers that have an even chance as active subjects to employ regulative speech acts, that is, to command and to resist, to allow and to forbid, to make and retract a promise, to account for something and to owe an explanation, etc. Only complete reciproci-

ty of behavioral expectations that exclude privileges in
the sense of one-sided binding behavioral and evaluative
norms can guarantee that the formal even distribution of
chances to open and continue an address can actually be
used to suspend the constraints of reality and move to the
area of communication that is free from experience and
the burden of action.[35]

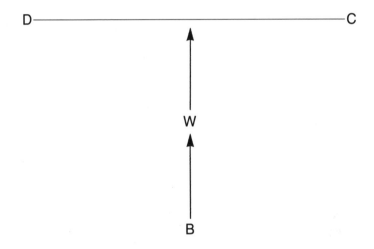

If these conditions for discourse are now settled, the question posed is one of discursive logic, which has to show where
the consensual attaining force of the argument lies. The logic of
the discourse must prepare the formal rules for argumentation
contexts. An argument, however, does not only consist of a series of sentences, but rather of a series of speech acts. "The transition will not (be able to) be founded exclusively logically" between such pragmatic units of speech, since we are not dealing
here with statements, but rather with engagements, that is, with
assertions and explanations, requirements or evaluations and
justifications." Furthermore, the transition from one speech act

to another cannot even be empirically founded "because in each case, the pragmatic units of speech have already interpreted their own specific relation to reality, whereas sentences must still be put in relation to reality."[36]

By means of discursive logic, the aptitude of an argument must be examined as to whether it serves to strengthen or weaken a validity claim. The validity claim is grounded in an argument; it should motivate us to recognize an assertion, a requirement or an evaluation. Arguments must be substantial: plausibility takes the place of logical continuity. In light of the formal structure of an argument, Habermas refers to the suggestion of Toulmin, which may be demonstrated in a diagram. (This diagram, and the next as well, are taken from the essay "Truth Theories.")

> The assertion "This stone fell to the earth" is the *conclusion* (C). This assertion must be explained by a reason: "Galileo dropped it from the tower" (D = *data*). In a next step, by means of a general law, we must identify this explanatory reason through an axiom as a reliable deduction, which in this example here is the law of falling bodies: W = *warrant*. Now comes what is really of importance for discursive logic: the proof of the plausibility of the general axiom. Here, the proof is the casuistic evidence of the law of falling bodies, known as *backing* (B), and thus, the inductive proof of the law. In discursive logic, we only determine an argument to be cogent when it "is *possible* in the sense of discursive modalities. This is the case if no deductive relationship exists between B and W, and if at the same time B is sufficient *motivation* to count W as plausible. We call substantial only those arguments that create plausibility under logical discontinuity, that is, in spite of a change in levels between B and W."[37] Only then can we see that, in a logical sense, an argument may be thoroughly discontinuous in discourse. The whole sequence is summarized as follows: first an "assertion in need of explanation or recommendation is brought into a deductive context with at least two other sentences; then the acceptability of the general statements (hypothetical laws, norms of behavior or critical evaluation) functioning as premises are supported through casuistic evidence. The consensus–building force of an argument rests on the transition from B to W justified by induction or universalization."[38]

Just as with the hypothetical laws in the natural sciences, a social norm can also be put into the form of a scientific problem. This happens when the argument is qualified as at variance and W is not recognized as a general law. If another norm is to take its place, it must be made plausible. If the appropriateness of the norm is to be confirmed, then the argument *structure* is the same as in the theoretical discourse. The recommendation (C) in need of justification is as follows: you should give back to Eric the $50 he lent you. Justification (D) is as follows: Eric only lent you the money. The behavioral norm (W) is: money that has been lent must be given back; or, a debtor is obligated to return funds to the creditor as determined by either case law or statute. The casuistic evidence that could support this behavioral norm (B): we may cite the consequences and ramifications of this norm (lending institution) for the fulfillment of generally accepted needs; i.e., one can make plausible that it is sensible for someone to satisfy his needs with a loan if he has no money at the moment.[39]

The substantial difference between practical and theoretical discourse is that in the case of theoretical discourse, the plausibility arguments cannot depend on reality (nature), while practical discourse is critical of social reality. Therefore, the transition here from backing to warrant must be a different one. It is not an inductive transition; rather, here only those norms are allowed (instead of natural laws in the theoretical discourse) that have general validity in their sphere of influence; all norms that claim particular validity are excluded. Thus, plausible arguments must also prove universal validity.[40]

The different steps to the argument are clear in a diagram (see p. 38).

Habermas cites freedom of movement between the different levels of discourse as a further condition for the vindication of a validity claim that can be examined discursively. This movement must be possible due to the formal structure of the discourse. This is especially important in one respect: an argument can only have consensus–building force when the argument is not only

	Theoretic-empirical Discourse	Practical Discourse
C	Assertions	Requirements/Bans
Controversial Validity Claim	Truth	Rightness/Appropriateness
Demanded by Discourse Partner	Explanations	Justifications
D	Causes (of Events) Motives (of Actions)	Grounds
W	Empirical Uniformity Hypothetical Laws	Behavioral/Evaluative Norms or Principles
B	Observations, Results of Questioning, Assessments, etc.	Details of Interpreted Needs (Values), Consequences, Ramifications, etc.

supported by a linguistic system bound by fixed rules, but also when this linguistic system itself can be discussed in the discourse. This is so since the way we describe reality with linguistic systems is development dependent. We must be able to pursue this cognitive development in discourse if we are to determine that the linguistic system we find does not allow for an appropriate description of reality. Thus, one must also be able to change the level of discourse in order to move to the level of a substantial linguistic criticism should the need arise.

> Progress in recognition occurs in the form of a substantial linguistic criticism. An argumentatively attained consensus may then, and only then, be viewed as a criterion for reality if structurally the possibility exists to analyze, to modify and to replace the respective *grounded* language in which experiences are interpreted.[41]

This last step leads to yet another discursive level, namely, the basic criticism of knowledge. With this the question may be posed in theoretical discourse: "How shall we gain cognitive accomplishments that can make a claim to the title knowledge?"[42] Since knowledge measures itself equally by that which shall be known as well as by the interest which must greet it, the argument goes in both directions. In practical discourse we must reflect on the dependence of the need structures from the position of knowledge and ability. The question is: "What shall we want to know?"[43]

The levels of discourse at our disposal again may be shown in a diagram (see p. 40).

In summary: truth and appropriateness are validity claims in the communicative area. Only when a communication no longer functions, when these validity claims become problematic for one or several communication participants and are no longer simply recognized, then truth or appropriateness are available to us in discourse. Discourse must fulfill quite specific conditions: the question of the competence of discourse participants is settled through

Step of Radicalization	Theoretical Discourse	Practical Discourse
Actions	Assertions	Requirements/Bans
Grounds	Theoretical Explanations	Theoretical Justifications
Substantial Linguistic Criticism	Metatheoretical	Metaethical/Metapolitical
	Changes of Linguistic and Conceptual Systems	
Self-reflection	Criticism of Cognition	Development of an Informed Opinion

the introduction of the ideal speech situation; a special logic for discourse is introduced by Habermas; and the condition of the free movement between levels of discourse is elucidated.

The three validity claims—truth, rightness or appropriateness, and truthfulness—"converge in a single one: that of sensibleness,"[44] which brings us to the subject of our next chapter. Habermas once said in an interview that reason should "show in its unity the instances of reason that were taken apart in all three Kantian criticisms: the unity of theoretical reason with moral-practical insight and aesthetic power of judgement."[45] Here we find again the validity claims: theoretical reason formulates the truth, practical reason the appropriateness, and the aesthetic-expressive instance of reason the truthfulness. It becomes clear through another remark made in the same interview that Habermas reaches back here to the insights of Kant when he postulates the unity of reason. After he got used to the neo-Kantian language, he was "somehow relieved." He could now more simply express what he thought.[46]

In this respect, the Habermasian position can be illuminated best in a philosophical-historic way. Relative to the development of the concept of enlightenment, today we see that Habermas stands at the end of a chain of development that began in ancient Greece.

3

HABERMAS'S RECONSTRUCTION OF REASON

THE HISTORIC SELF-DIFFERENTIATION OF REASON

The philosophy of ancient Greece had two great themes: the problem of the *arche* or the origin—which has been equated with the issue of nature and truth at least since the time of Aristotle—and the problem of thought, or *nous*, which can probably be translated as "reason."[1] For the pre-Socratic period we may accept the perspective of Parmenides, in which existence and thought, and truth and reason are the same. Today the world view of the Greeks is beyond our understanding. For our purposes, however, we can assume that the pre-Socratics believed that existence constitutes unity as such. This unity is the fundamental one that unites all individual existences, as well as all individual perceptions. The perceptible diversity forms a unity for thought, and not simply because reason and truth are the same thing; reason creates unity for the simple reason that it is unity. Relative to Kant, we must speak of the "unity of consciousness."[2] Reason has not yet been split into the three instances that Habermas found in Kant, but not yet in Plato. Günther Patzig is absolutely right when he says,

"Plato was the first thinker in European history who attempted to discuss in detail and resolve knowledge-theoretical, ontological, ethical and aesthetic questions on the basis of a unified theory, namely the theory of ideas."[3]

As far as I can tell, the development of the self-differentiation of reason in its three instances has its first barely perceptible germination with Aristotle. This idea is suggested in the discussion of the highest virtue. Is intelligence or wisdom the highest virtue? Intelligence is present when—in contemporary terminology—the practical instance of reason coincides with the theoretical. The knowledge of intelligence is inseparably tied to ethos: "Virtue helps one to set the correct goal, and intelligence to choose the correct means."[4] Here we can still see that a reasonable virtue must be very closely tied to an ethical one, and must even interact with it. Nonetheless, for Aristotle there is still a virtue, which he calls wisdom, that exists for itself alone. Aristotle tells us that there was a science conducted by the Egyptians that was a goal in and of itself and was in no way mediated with practical needs, nor did it provide any instructions. Those who conducted this science were called philosophers; philosophy means love of wisdom.

Thus, if it is true for Aristotle that wisdom is the highest virtue, then we already have an instance of a separation of theoretical and practical reason. Actually, in viewing Aristotle's works, we see that we can often speak of a kind of science liberated from values. On the other hand, when we look at his treatment of intelligence, we see that the break between science and morality has not yet been completely achieved. Although science is granted an independence from practical questions, morality and science are nevertheless extremely closely connected. Habermas believes that this divergence of morality and science, which, I believe, is first evidenced in Aristotle, increases in the course of history.

This burgeoning independence of science initially was not continued in the Christian way of thinking during the Middle Ages. St. Augustine preserved unity by means of the concept that the unified foundation for knowledge, and at the same time for the rightful order of life, was to be found in God. After St. Augustine, according to the Book of John, one could only act truth, and not think it. With St. Thomas Aquinas also, in spite of the differences between theoretical and practical reason made by Aquinas following Aristotle, the rules for the respective use of reason may be derived from unified foundations of reason.

This unity of reason was born by the church, a strong power that had proved itself in the struggle with Rome, the world power at the time. But a power like the church, however, invited opposition. Thus, the unity of reason started to crack when the writings of Aristotle became known via the Arab world in the twelfth and thirteenth centuries. In 1210 the study of these writings was forbidden because they contained scientific truths that conflicted with the revelatory truths of the Bible. In 1277 the Bishops of Paris accused the scientists representing Aristotle's theories of assuming two truths: revelatory truths and scientific truths. However, the advancement of the insights of the secular scientists could not be held back. With Habermas one can speak of an autonomy relative to the sciences. On the other hand, in the Middle Ages the "pious criticism of the arrogance of knowledge and the ignorance of the learned"[5] demanded either a return to the Holy Book and its simple truths or an abandonment of rationality in order to obey the "simplicity of the heart."[6] These warnings were fruitless. Representatives of the church such as the Franciscan Wilhelm von Ockham, for example, were increasingly influential, and for longer periods of time. Ockham traced metaphysical phenomena back to empirical evidence; regarding his science, it was superfluous to refer back to the essential groundings of things or to the ideas of God.

In modern times, this tendency toward divergence of the different instances of reason referred to by Habermas becomes increasingly more stable. Initially human reason is still in the image of God. But in short order Nicolaus Cusanus heralds the new development that man is the measure of all things, and that he is required "under definitive renunciation of all attempts to seek the foundation of truth in other areas outside of the *mens* [human mind] itself, and to decide for himself alone and determine what certainty, knowledge and truth mean."[7] The self-examination of reason remained unconcluded for approximately another three hundred years—Descartes, for example, attempted to derive the unity of ontological knowledge and ethical knowledge from a single foundation, a *mathesis universalis* [8]—until Immanuel Kant analyzed this development of thought and subjected it to a fundamental critique. He showed that the different domains of the world are interpreted with different rules, each of which is assigned to a particular instance of reason. The objective domain is interpreted with the rules of theoretical reason that are founded in the *Critique of Pure Reason*; the social domain with the rules of practical reason (*Critique of Practical Reason*), and the subjective domain with the rules of aesthetic-expressive reason that are laid out in *Critique of Judgement*. It is often overlooked (even Habermas does not give this point enough consideration) that Kant was intent on presenting the three instances of reason in a unity in which the practical instance of reason has primacy.[9]

Since Kant, the differentiation of the three instances of reason has come noticeably to the fore. Philosophic-historically it is an absolutely essential development that a philosopher has posed the question of whether connecting lines may not still be found against the so clearly perceptible separation of the instances of reason. Habermas poses this question, and he analyzes the relationship of the three instances of reason to one another.

THE INTEGRATION OF THE INSTANCES OF REASON AND CRITICAL SOCIAL THEORY

We live in a complex society in which the separation of theoretical and practical reason has asserted itself as the product of historical development. In his *Theory of Communicative Action* it is

Habermas's intent to illuminate this complex world in a social analysis based on a theory of rationality. Where he attempts to analyze the rationalization process that inaugurates and characterizes modernity, even on the level of a rationality inherent to communicative action, the results of his language-analytical works fold during the examination. Moreover, Habermas reaches back comprehensively to antecedent sociological and social-philosophical theory formation, from which he reconstructs elements of a social analysis that are contained in all theory, inasmuch as theory itself evolved upon social constellations.

His understanding gets its direction above all in the great social philosophy of Max Weber, from which Habermas critically distances himself at the same time. Weber's investigations probe the origin and significance of occidental rationality, which for him is the hallmark of modernity. Weber describes the profanization of culture through the disenchantment of mythical-religious worldviews as a process of rationalization; similarly, the development of modern societies toward the distinction between capitalist enterprise and state apparatus is a process of rationalization, as well. According to Habermas, however, Weber's approach falls short in that he simply follows the pattern of capitalistic rationalization and one-sidedly singles out the dimension of purposive-rational action.

This critique of Max Weber leads Habermas to a change in paradigm from purposive-rational to communicative action.

> The phenomena in need of explication are no longer, in and of themselves, the knowledge and mastery of an objective nature, but the intersubjectivity of possible understanding and agreement—at both the interpersonal and intrapsychic levels. The focus of investigation thereby shifts from cognitive-instrumental rationality to communicative rationality. And what is paradigmatic for the latter is not the relation of a solitary subject to something in the objective world that can be represented and manipulated, but the intersubjective relation that speaking and acting subjects take up when they come to an understanding with one another about something. In doing so, communicative actors move in the

medium of a natural language, draw upon culturally transmitted
interpretations, and relate simultaneously to something in the one
objective world, something in their common social world, and
something in each's own subjective world.[10]

In so doing, the communicative actors hereby establish three
validity claims simultaneously. If they convey something about
the *objective* world, they establish a truth claim; they refer to the
social world with a *normative rightness claim*; they return to the
subjective world with a truthfulness claim. Contrary to the assumption of Max Weber, they always act on three levels of rationality.

Now one might assume that the idea of truth may be particularistic or relativistic since it is always formulated in a "culturally determined" setting, which itself is contained in the languages used to make the truth claim. Habermas states that the
lifeworld and communicative action serve to complement one
another. This effect, however, in no way contradicts the thesis
of the universal truth claim put forward by Habermas: "All languages provide the possibility to distinguish between that which
is true and that which we hold to be true. The assumption of a
common objective world is built into the pragmatics of every use
of language."[11] This has the consequence that a true statement
"merits universal assent, no matter in which language it is formulated."[12]

Given this change in paradigm from purposive-rational to
communicative action that results from the critical analysis of Max
Weber's work, it may be demonstrated that sociated people always move on three levels of rationality. Habermas proves this
decentering or self-differentiation of reason in its three instances
with the help of ethnological investigations. Primarily following
George Herbert Mead, he shows how symbolically mediated interaction arises from gesture-mediated interaction,[13] and how a
meaning convention develops in the process.[14] Habermas finds
Mead to be overly hasty when he proceeds "abruptly from symbolically mediated to normatively regulated action," neglecting
the path that leads to a "differentiated communication in lan-

guage."[15] Habermas follows this path after studying the work of Emile Durkheim, and he comes to the following conclusion:

> The rationality potential in action oriented to mutual understanding can be released and translated into the rationalization of the lifeworlds of social groups to the extent that language fulfills functions of reaching understanding, coordinating actions, and socializing individuals. It thereby becomes a medium through which cultured reproduction, social integration and socialization take place.[16]

According to Habermas, Mead also shows very little of how norms develop from symbolically mediated interaction. In order to fill this gap in the development of the very important practical level of rationality with its normative rightness claim, here again Habermas reaches back to Durkheim: "To the degree that the rationality potential ingrained in communicative action is released, the archaic core of the normative dissolves and gives way to the rationalization of worldviews, to the universalization of law and morality, and to an acceleration of processes of individuation."[17] (I will return again to these processes of individuation in the third section of this chapter.) In this context Habermas uses Durkheim's observation that the aura of the sacred changes into the validity of moral rules. With the rationalization of societies, the holy is superseded by rational legal rules.[18] "The aura of rapture and terror that emanates from the sacred, the *spellbinding* power of the holy, is sublimated into the *binding/bonding* force of criticizable validity claims and at the same time turned into an everyday occurrence. . . . Like Weber, Durkheim conceived of legal development as a process of disenchantment."[19] Durkheim speaks of the rule of reflection; he means the "achievement of mutual understanding by a communication community of citizens, their own words, that brings about the binding consensus."[20]

After Habermas demonstrated the development to a differentiated linguistic communication, he wants to show in *The Theory of Communicative Action* how systems form in developed societies; systems that profess goals so that only the means must be sought to attain these goals. Subsequent to pointing out the development of the practical level of rationality, this is an important aspect because the development here continues to systems. Habermas argues as follows: the lifeworld is the "horizon-forming context of processes of reaching understanding"[21] in which the entire stock of cultural, social and personality-forming knowledge is reflected.[22] Societies that are becoming increasingly complex must attempt to avoid two dangers in the lifeworld: "the risk of not coming to some understanding, that is, of disagreement or misunderstanding, and the risk of a plan of action miscarrying, that is, of failure."[23] The risk of misunderstanding is checked by the mass media (print, press, electronic media), and the risk of a failed plan of action by steering media (media like money and power). The communication media remain bound to the lifeworld context; they generalize communication, free it from the "provinciality of spatiotemporally restricted contexts" and allow a great public sphere to form that is not spatiotemporally bound and whose messages are "available for manifold contexts."[24]

The media of money and power, however, are able to become autonomous with respect to the lifeworld. Thus, we can see the advantage provided by these media in that they unburden the process of communication and social consensus building: we no longer need to haggle over the price or give administrative instructions for all clear and valid orders. However, there is the danger that the media of money and power may become autonomous and strike back;[25] thus Habermas is forced to conclude that "a progressively rationalized lifeworld is both uncoupled from and made dependent upon increasingly complex, formally organized domains of action, like the economy and the state administration."[26] Habermas speaks of a "monetarization and bureaucratization of everyday practices."[27] Our society today has reached this historic point.

In summary, then, we may say that from our contemporary standpoint, cultural-historical development is to be seen both as a process of the increasing divergence of the three instances of reason, as well as the growing development of subsystems of purposive-rational action.[28] This statement—and Habermas is aware of this—succeeds only "in the horizon of a modern understanding of the world."[29]

Faced with this development, as we saw in the first chapter, Habermas does not sink into resignation like Weber or Horkheimer and Adorno. Instead, he asserts that the world can be changed, including the steering media that are part of it, since these are ultimately bound to the communicative everyday life by means of the fundamental institutions of civil or public law.[31] As Habermas sees it, only when one is well acquainted with the nature of the current crisis can one decide how a change in the current social situation can be possible. As we saw, the communicative infrastructure today is threatened by two tendencies. First, expert cultures are forming in the fields of science, art and art criticism, morality and jurisprudence; these specialists detach themselves from communicative everyday life. Second, the subsystems, which are now self-sufficient, swing back to areas that "resist the alteration to the media of money and power."[31] It is precisely at these junctures that conflicts and social crises arise; however, within these conflicts lies the hope for change in the lifeworld including its steering media. This hope for change is already expressed today in the real potential for protest. "Alternative practice is directed against the profit-dependent instrumentalization of work in one's vocation, the market-dependent mobilization of labor power, against the extension of pressures of competition and performance all the way down into elementary school. It also takes aim at the monetarization of services, relationships, and time, at the consumerist redefinition of private spheres of life and personal life-styles. Furthermore, the relation of clients to public service agencies is to be opened up and reorganized in a participatory mode, along the lines of self-help organizations."[32]

The goal of protest that arises at the intersection of system
and lifeworld must be to answer the two questions of "(i) whether
a reason that has objectively split up into its moments can still
preserve its unity, and (ii) how expert cultures can be mediated
with everyday practice."[33] Thus, we must also become aware of
what we have "unlearned" in the course of our cultural learning
process[34] in order to allow alternative ideas to gain a consensus
and be put into social practice. Short term attempts at a solution
are doomed to failure; we see this simply by looking back at the
developmental history of the problem, which goes back a long
way. The self-differentiation of reason and the rationalization of
the lifeworld have led so far that the goals and significance of
action can no longer be pulled into lifeworld communication and
determined according to the rules of practical reason by those
who are themselves taking part; instead these goals are determined by the independent steering media. This kind of rationalized action has gained adequate expression in the form of eco-
logical crisis and a life-threatening arms buildup. It finds its orientation according to institutionalized and unquestioned values that
simply serve to set a quantitative measure: increase in the avail-
ability of man and nature, profit maximization. The splitting of
reason and the suppression of its practical-moral element turns
into destruction.

Social-political action in this day and age is founded above
all on the insights provided by theoretical reason. For example,
governmental action directs itself according to economic actualities and administrative facts. Habermas speaks here of a "colonization of the lifeworld." These findings could also come from Weber's analysis or the theory of the older Frankfurt School. For
Habermas, however, their rationalization concepts fall short of
the mark. From his own sophisticated work, he found that models
of communicative action show how the three instances of reason are still cryptically tied to each other, in spite of their separation. Every pronouncement on the objective world also contains
a reference to something in the subjective, or social, world. To

be sure, this connection of the three instances of reason is only vestigially present; it must be taken up and shaped into a real unity.

If one follows the Habermasian analysis, the attitude of so-ciated man as a whole would have to change in order to allow for the alleviation of social misery. People can only prohibit catas-trophe if they understand and are put in a position to accept the responsibility for social processes themselves, and no longer al-low themselves to be influenced by situations that are propagat-ed by institutions. Here we necessarily come upon the relation-ship of individual and society and the problem of moral foundation.

HABERMASIAN GROUNDING OF MORALITY

In order to be able to analyze the relationship of individual and society in our culture, in his book *The Philosophical Discourse of Modernity,* Jürgen Habermas returns to Hegel's definition of the subject:

> Hegel sees the modern age as marked universally by . . . . subjec-tivity. . . . [T]he principle of subjectivity determines the forms of modern culture. This holds true first of all for objectifying science. . . . The moral concepts of modern times follow from the recognition of the subjective freedom of individuals. . . . Modern art reveals its essence in Romanticism; and absolute inwardness determines the form and content of Romantic art. . . . In moder-nity, therefore, religious life, state, and society as well as science, morality and art are transformed into just so many embodiments of the principle of subjectivity.[35]

The ensuing question that is forever asked in the philosophi-cal discourse of modernity is whether the principle of subjectivi-ty suffices as the source of normative orientations.

> The question now is whether one can obtain from subjectivity and self-consciousness criteria that are taken from the modern world and are at the same time fit for orienting oneself within it—and

this also means fit for the critique of a modernity that is at variance with itself.[36]

Habermas pursues this question, as well as the issue of how
the relationship of the individual subject to the whole should be
conceived.

As Habermas sees it, Marx, who viewed the troubled relation of individual and collective as his central theme, could not
satisfactorily answer the question of how the individual could ab-
sorb the citizen into himself. Moreover, according to Habermas,
in this respect Hegel completely overloaded the concept of subject. The "self-sufficient subjectivity that is posited absolutely"[37]
becomes unconditional. It would have to be demonstrated,
however, that subjectivity itself is conditioned and correlated to
intersubjectivity. The detachment of subjectivity from intersubjectivity is also the reason why Hegel could "not obtain the aspect
of reconciliation—that is, the reestablishment of the disintegrat-
ed totality—from self-consciousness or the reflective relationship
of the knowing subject to itself."[38]

In reconstructing *The Philosophical Discourse of Modernity*,
Habermas criticizes the philosophers who follow Hegel down this
path all the way through Adorno, Horkheimer, Heidegger, Der-
rida, Bataille, Foucault, Castoriadis and Luhmann. I will not go
into detail on Habermas's critique here. His constructive approach
is founded on the work of George Herbert Mead. According to
Habermas, the problem of subjectivity and intersubjectivity lapses
"as soon as linguistically generated intersubjectivity gains primacy."[39] Mead was of the opinion—as I pointed out in the second
chapter—that the entire social structure is formed through language; language contains everything that is necessary for the construction of a society and the functioning interaction of the members of the society that is tied to it (customs, cultural traditions,
self-evident moral tenets, technical skills, etc.). According to Mead,
language is the medium that pulls in all interactive participants
into the communication community; it sociates individuals. In this
way the individual learns the orientations and rules of communal

life and secures them, as well. At the same time, language subjects the members of a society to a pressure to individuate via the system of personal pronouns. Thus, Mead was of the opinion that the socialization of an individual occurs in a reciprocal and simultaneous process with social development. In the same way, society is formed along with the individual. According to Habermas, Mead's theory has the advantage that it is based on actualities: "Because such reconstructive attempts are no longer aimed at a realm of the intelligible beyond that of appearances, but at the actually exercised rule-knowledge that is deposited in correctly generated utterances, the ontological separation between the transcendental and the empirical is no longer applicable."[40] Thus, with this step, the contradiction perceived by Hegel and the philosophers that followed him, was overcome.

When one follows Habermas in the transition from the paradigm of the philosophy of consciousness to the paradigm of understanding,

> the sort of objectifying attitude that an observer assumes toward entities in the external world [is no longer privileged]. The transcendental-empirical doubling of the relation to self is only unavoidable so long as there is no alternative to this observer-perspective; only then does the subject have to view itself as the dominating counterpart to the world as a whole or as an entity appearing within it.[41]

With this transition from the philosophy of consciousness to the philosophy of language, the analysis of self-consciousness via the reconstruction of the competencies of speaking, acting and knowing subjects becomes possible. What is the consequence for the grounding of morality?

> The further the structures of a lifeworld become differentiated, the more clearly we can see how the growing self-determination of the individuated person is crossed with the mounting integration into multiplied social dependencies. The further the individualization progresses, the further the individual subject is woven

into an increasingly thicker and at the same time more subtle net of reciprocal defenselessness and exponential need for protection.[42]

The task of morality finds its proportions according to this relation of individuation and sociating intersubjectivity; in the same way it must secure the unimpeachability of the individuals and the structures of an intersubjectively shared lifeworld. But how can discourse ethics dissolve these two tasks into one? This is now the decisive question.

Discourse ethics takes up the question posed by ethics of how moral commandments and norms may be grounded. As did Kant, discourse ethics proceeds from the capacity of norms to be generalized. All cognitivistic ethics comprehend "normative rightness. . . as a validity claim analogous to truth."[43] With Kant, the universalization principle is the requirement of the categorical imperative by which norms capable of generalization are measured. Discourse ethics attempt to base this principle in the framework of the paradigm of understanding. The categorical imperative reformulated linguistic-philosophically requires that the universalization tenet—as a moral principle—be tied to the process of moral argumentation: "It posits the tenet that only those norms that could meet with the approval of all affected as participants to a practical discourse may make a claim to validity."[44] Or, in other words, only those norms may attain general recognition, and thus, social validity—whose consequences will be borne by all affected—regardless of whether they will use the norm actively in a particular situation, or whether they would be passively affected by it at another time.[45] Habermas is able to provide the grounding for this moral principle by reverting back to the argumentation of universal pragmatics: "As a participant to an argumentation, an individual focuses on himself, but yet remains embedded in a universal context."[46] This is taken into account by the discourse rules that Karl-Otto Apel[47] reconstructed and that Habermas interprets as the universal facilitation of a situation of understanding on the discourse level.

Practical discourse as a rigorous form of the argumentative development of an informed opinion can guarantee the correctness of a normative consensus solely on the basis of "the idealizing assumptions that the participants must actually make in their argumentation praxes."[48] Due to the formal character of the discourse, each individual who undertakes the discursive vindication of normative validity claims is already tied to the conditions of the proceedings, which is equal to recognition of the generalization principle. In practical discourse, disputed norms only meet with approval if the rules of discourse are obeyed.

> The discursively attained agreement at the same time depends on the "yeah" or "nay" of each individual, for which there is no substitute, as well as the individual being able to overcome his egocentric perspective. Without the unrestricted individual freedom to make criticizable validity claims, a factually attained agreement cannot be truly common; without the united sympathy of each for the situation of all others, a solution that meets with common approval is not possible. The method of discursive opinion-development takes into account the internal context of both aspects—the autonomy of unrepresentable individuals and their embeddedness in intersubjectively shared life forms. The same individual rights and equal observance of their personal worth is carried by a nexus of interpersonal relations and relations of reciprocal recognition.[49]

At this point, the difficult issue of the universal rightness or appropriateness claim appears, which Habermas intentionally omits.[50] The universal rightness claim must be viewed in analogy with the universal truth claim. Habermas focuses on the transition from the process of grounding to application: in effect, each universalistic morality depends on accommodating life forms, just as, conversely, moral universality is first formed in societies with corresponding traits.

> Without such testaments of an (albeit in fragments and splinters, nevertheless) "existing reason," the moral intuitions that bring discourse ethics to even arrive at the term would not have been able

to form, at least not in their full breadth. On the other hand, the step by step embodiment of moral tenets in concrete life forms is not something that one should entrust to the course of the absolute intellect, as Hegel does. Above all, this phenomenon owes its existence to the collective efforts and sacrifices of social and political movements. Even philosophy may not feel itself removed from the historic dimension to which these movements belong.[51] To be sure, philosophy can relieve "nobody of practical responsibility!"[52]

CHAPTER

4

THE EROSION OF
WESTERN CULTURE
JÜRGEN HABERMAS'S
MAGNUM OPUS
by William van Reijen

It is somewhat risky to use the term *magnum opus* on the occasion of the publication of a new book by such a productive and relatively young philosopher as Jürgen Habermas, even when the oeuvre in question is a two volume work consisting of a total of 1200 pages. Nonetheless, the *Theory of Communicative Action* is without a doubt a milestone—for Habermas himself and certainly also for philosophers, sociologists, and all others involved in the human sciences, either directly or indirectly. This extensive work views society as a patient and makes a diagnosis. To be more precise, it analyzes the causes and consequences of the destructive forces that threaten the human lifeworld.

Habermas believes that today the primary threat to man and society is not economic exploitation (the assumption of Marx) or political dictatorships and ideologies (the assertion of early critical theory at the time of fascism), but rather the encroachment of bureaucratic authorities in social relationships which will lose their characteristic human qualities and become formalized. He calls this process the "colonization of the lifeworld." Habermas's work leads him to formulate a social theory based upon

> a theory of modernity that explains the type of social pathologies that are today becoming increasingly visible, by way of the assumption that communicatively structured domains of life are being subordinated to the imperatives of autonomous, formally organized systems of action.[1]

In his study Habermas uses the most significant sociological and philosophical approaches to date, and he goes far afield. Weber, Durkheim, Parsons, ethnomethodology, and symbolic interactionism are combined with phenomenology and philosophy of language, with Piaget and Kohlberg into one great synthesis. Marx and Lukács get a chance to speak, as do Adorno and Horkheimer. And Habermas makes use of his own earlier work, even if he now modifies some of it in not insignificant ways. There is no philosopher of the past or present who synthesizes anywhere near the number of different theoretical approaches Habermas combines, and it is not surprising that he was earlier accused of eclecticism.

This reproach, however, can easily be refuted. Habermas does not simply throw different scientific systems of thought together; rather, in every respect, he shows exactly what we can learn from different sociologists and philosophers for a better understanding of the current situation, as well as where weak points in their theories lie.[2] Naturally, this does not preclude the fact that one may differ in opinion with Habermas about the way in which the sociologists and philosophers he refers to should be interpreted. Since our future, however, is "open," the reference to different modes of interpretation is, so to speak, a triviality.

More interesting is the conclusion that even if Habermas's interpretations of, say, Weber and Parsons deviate in part or even in great measure from the current academic interpretations, this does not harm the logical consistency of his argumentation. In order to concretize this point, and at the same time introduce the construction and content of the *Theory of Communicative Action*, I would like to turn to Habermas's central thesis in order to show how he substantiates it.

DIAGNOSIS OF SOCIETY

Habermas concludes that the greatest threat to society (with the exception of questions of political security, in which he does not engage) lies in the destruction of specifically human communication structures by an ever expanding bureaucracy. As an example of "the trend toward juridification of informally regulated spheres of the lifeworld,"[3] Habermas points to the increasing intervention of politics, laws and bureaucratic authorities into family life. Thus, children are confronted at ever younger ages with school and education; they are becoming the object of legal rulings increasingly early (they can refer earlier and/or more often to social help in the case of a conflict with parents, etc.).

> In fact, however, in these spheres of the lifeworld, we find, prior to any juridification, norms and contexts of action that by fundamental necessity are based on mutual understanding as a mechanism for coordinating action.[4]

Habermas certainly does not deny that political regulation is necessary to a certain degree—certainly in the case of a conflict—but he sees a tendency to make human relationships the object of bureaucratic measures "wherever the traditionalist padding of capitalist modernization has worn through."[5] Communication, however, comprises mainly co-existence on the basis of agreement on the validity of certain opinions and rules. Habermas creates the concept of the lifeworld as a complement to communicative action.

> Correspondingly, a lifeworld can be regarded as rationalized to the extent that it permits interactions that are not guided by nor-

matively ascribed agreement but—directly or indirectly—by communicatively achieved understanding.[6]

In all instances where the state intervenes in human relationships, certain aspects—according to Habermas, the essential ones—are disregarded. The bureaucratic treatment of relationships requires that complex phenomena be reduced to "cases" that can be understood according to one simple rule. On the basis of the example cited (and I would like to emphasize that we are dealing with an example), Habermas shows how politics, the administration of justice and the economy in general function. A preoccupation with efficiency and purposiveness spreads; Habermas calls this phenomenon means/ends rationality.

Habermas sees a similar development in the social sciences that make use of political decision-making, and in the process they fall under the spell of means/ends rationality also. Nevertheless, in the face of this relatively modest, not particularly new social-philosophical point of view, one might ask himself if we are not shooting at sparrows with cannons, so to speak. Is this whole arsenal of theories really necessary for the analysis of the issue here? In order to answer this question and then be able to decide if Habermas himself is being fair to one of the requirements of scientific assertions, namely, not to use more theoretical assumptions than necessary (but also not fewer than necessary!) we must consider the subject of Habermas's work: communicative action.

In communicative action, according to Habermas, three aspects may be distinguished that appear in all instances where humans act together, if not in equal measure. First, people coordinate actions (in the production of goods, for example, but actually in all instances where people work together toward a goal and on the basis of a certain division of labor). The judgement of such behavior occurs on the basis of its success or failure. Second, humans act on the basis of norms (opinions on good and evil) about which agreement has already been reached or must be reached during the action. This type of action cannot succeed or fail, but rather may be judged solely on the basis of its accordance (or lack thereof) with the prevailing norms. Third, in all actions people show something of their inner condition, of their intentions, needs, fears, etc. Motives of this kind may be misrepresented, and it remains beyond question that some people know how to express their situations better than others; but from different utterances and the agreement between deeds and words, we can succeed in drawing conclusions relative to truthfulness.

> However, the knowledge embodied in normatively regulated actions or in expressive manifestations does not refer to the existence of states of affairs but to the validity of norms or to the manifestation of subjective experiences.[7]

COMMUNICATIVE RATIONALITY AS THE CRUX

The crux of Habermas's explanation lies in the assertion that language plays a decisive role, both in the coordination of actions as well as in normative (or, if one so chooses, ethical) judgement including its justifications and the ascertainment of the truthfulness (or lack thereof) of our assertions. For Habermas, the "process of humanization" is not founded in the conscious production of the necessities of life (Marx) or in the use of tools (Rousseau), but rather in the use of language. Habermas seeks to develop the idea of communicative rationality by introducing the concept of linguistically coming to an understanding.

> This concept of communicative rationality carries with it connotations based ultimately on the central experience of the unconstrained, unifying, consensus—bringing force of argumentative speech, in which different participants overcome their merely subjective views and, owing to the mutuality of rationally motivated conviction, assure themselves of both the unity of the objective world and the intersubjectivity of their lifeworld.[8]

Habermas, in his recourse to language, is following along the path cleared by the founder of symbolic interactionism, George Herbert Mead. Mead asserted that the development of speech and self-consciousness are steadfastly bound to one another and are only possible in a social context. For Habermas, this is important because he believes that the second aspect of communicative action, the normative judgement of actions, in a way represents the most comprehensive model of human action. More pronouncedly than with other aspects, here humans create their reality themselves. In other words, they are not subject to the limitations imposed upon them "from without" (nature) or "from within" (unavoidable physical and psychic needs). Instead, here humans act (although within historically cultural boundaries) confidently and autonomously. To use Habermas's wording, they can say yes or no, and in so doing, change social reality. This change occurs in a concrete way in which again and again an understanding is reached about the validity of certain norms. In this process language not only plays a fundamental role because it is the last medium of control that examines the intentions, expectations and action viewpoints of the other, but above all because certain criteria underlie the use of language, without which the use of language itself, and along with it every form of action, would be senseless.

Linguistic action is for Habermas the ultimate model of action. "The concept of reaching an understanding suggests a rationally motivated agreement among participants that is measured against criticizable validity claims."[9] That which is said must be true; normative implications must be accepted as right; and finally, the truthfulness of the speaker must be presupposed. If we had to assume that most people generally lie (that their statements do not agree with the facts) and that which they say is not right in a moral light (that their and my moral convictions do not at all agree) and finally, that everybody always behaves in a cynical way, then in light of the three dimensions of action described previously, language would lose its mission, and understanding would be impossible. In this short explanation, we must emphasize that Habermas views these three requisites as ideal requisites whose principal vindication we assume in the transition from communicative action to discourse, where the validity claims are explicitly defined. On the level of discourse again, in principle we assume the principal potential for a situation in which an agreement may be reached, and in which each systematic distortion is excluded.

However abstract all of the preceding may appear at first glance, Habermas allows for no doubts about one thing: the model shown lies at the foundation of the Western form of democracy. It provides for advice and decision-making for the general good without making use of an informational advantage, the status of the speaker, not to mention other forms of power or exercise of force. The decision of the majority, which is accepted by the minority as binding for its own action, is only the temporary bridge that works on the basis of this so-called "consensus principle."

PURPOSIVE RATIONALITY AND VALUE RATIONALITY (Max Weber)

By means of the fundamental analysis that Habermas prepared in numerous essays and the chapters of earlier works, he can now pursue two secondary questions: which course has our Western cultural and political development taken and which aspects have been illuminated by sociology and social philosophy, and where have we run into the trap of one-sidedness?

Behind the posing of these questions is the view that the three dimensions of action and the claims of truth—normative appropriateness and truthfulness that are tied to them—originally constituted a unity. The real meaning of the term rationality is found in this unity. The connecting thread of Habermas's explanation is the idea that a one-sided orientation toward purposive and truth criteria manifested itself in the course of the development, and that in the process, aspects of ethics and truthfulness were pushed to the margin.

At the same time, an alteration of terms took place. The term rationality is now used exclusively in the sense of a means/ends rationality. Due to this change, one "forgets" that rationality actually includes more. However, if we succeed in gaining an insight into the causes and the context of our historical development, it can also be explained that historical events are not a destiny, but rather may be guided by human beings. The basic issue is "the question of whether, and if so how, capitalist modernization can be conceived as a process of one-sided rationalization."[10]

In his analysis of our sociocultural development, Habermas follows the paths of Max Weber and Emile Durkheim. Weber comes to the conclusion that at the beginning of our Western culture, people expressed their relations to one another and also their natural environment in myths and religious interpretations. Characteristic of the "narratives" and the life experience expressed within them is that there is no distinction between facts and fantasy, between word (sign or symbol) and that which is referred to, between one's own (individual) needs, drives and fears and social and natural events. Even an individual and personal consciousness is unknown.

Over time the process reaches the point that Weber calls disenchantment. Mythological and religious interpretations of the natural and social events lose their power. People learn to separate certain things. The question of truth becomes separate from that of moral rightness. Individual action can be distinguished from group action and (even later) from the actions of bureaucratic authorities. People learn that there are different orientations of action: for example an orientation toward efficiency criteria and one toward value criteria (or purposive rationality and value rationality).

Weber describes as rational the process of the differentiation of cultural value spheres—science, art, moral and legal theory. According to Weber, probably the most important thing is that humans can now act in a very focused way and with optimal use of the tools available to them. The enormous progress in the field of the taming of nature and the production of goods may only be explained as follows; comparing our Western culture with other cultures in which this division has taken place to a lesser degree.

Weber explains societal rationalization in the development of modern capitalism and the bureaucratic apparatus of the state. Weber sees in modern capitalism an adequate form of organization for a social system that values efficiency as highly as we do, and he conspicuously confirms a connection between the "systematic individual lifestyle"—which consists of an attitude that is oriented according to reality, weighs out ends and means, and makes use of broadly accepted social norms (the Protestant ascetic way of life) and the sphere of action available in the political system.

> Corresponding to cultural rationalization, we find at the level of the personality system that methodical conduct of life whose motivational bases were the chief object of Weber's interest because he believed himself to be grasping here a—if not the—most important factor in the rise of capitalism.[11]

Weber discovers many benefits in the differentiation of economy, jurisprudence and politics, which all function in the form of autonomous organizations and institutions with their own rules and laws and, thus, are better able to deal with specific problems without coming in conflict with one another in the process. Even if this advantage has become more dubious with the passing of time, it cannot be denied that the capacity to solve problems through the differentiation of distinct spheres of action is, in fact, primarily magnified.

Nevertheless, Weber also notices the disadvantage of this development. The uncoupling of effectiveness criteria from problems of justification results in a disorientation; success blinds people. Problems of justification are transformed into problems of method (formal conformity). As regards content, whether or not something is right becomes translated into the question of whether a solution (i.e., in the administration of justice) has emerged in the correct way. Nevertheless, Weber believes the orientation of means/ends rationality to be so important that he lays the foundation for a narrowing of the concept of rationality, so to speak.

According to Habermas, Weber identifies means/ends rationality with rationality in general, and in so doing, denies himself the possibility to use the "meaning" of action as the object of his sociology. Weber had "so biased" the question of an evenly balanced embodiment of all three rationality complexes "[t]hrough its basic action-theoretic assumption . . . that processes of societal rationalization could come into view only from the standpoint of purposive rationality."[12]

According to Habermas, Weber sees the dimension of action coordination and values above all the areas where this coordination can occur without the use of language or is "speechless," namely, economy and administration. Money and power are the media for the efficient compact on actions, intentions and criteria. Their legitimation lies in their function. The fact that they function in a non-linguistic way not only excludes the question of other criteria like "does it work?" but it does not even allow the question of the shortcomings of this criterion to be raised.

Here Habermas raises the fundamental question of whether money and power can function as social agents of cohesion—in other words, if the integration of individual goals and valuations in a social framework can be achieved exclusively by means of rewards in money and power (participation of individuals in wealth and politics)—or if the social system must also embody a generally accepted value system. In technical terms: system integration or social integration?

> [T]here is a competition *not between the types of action* oriented to understanding and to success, but *between principles of societal integration* (between the mechanism of linguistic communication that is oriented to validity claims—a mechanism that emerges in increasing purity from the rationalization of the lifeworld) and those de-linguistified steering media through which systems of success-oriented action are differentiated out.[13]

THE SACRED AND LANGUAGE (Durkheim)

From Durkheim Habermas takes the opinion that in the early myths and religious interpretations, the sacred (sacral) and language still constitute a unity. This justification is tied to the understanding between different individuals which emerges in an essentially linguistic way; it cannot be sufficiently explained in concepts of functionality and formal conformity. In short, not everything that can be done may be done, and the result of a correct method may also be incorrect. Durkheim sees religious rituals as the embodiment of the principle that the validity of normative taboos is not derived from the negative consequences of violating them—which is the case with violations of technical rules and laws punished in the form of failure and sanctions—but rather from the value that the rules in and of themselves possess. The sacred, which is binding, and the consensus of the group about the value and the membership of the group all form a unity. As does Max Weber, Durkheim sees that social organization increasingly rejects an "intrinsic value" as an agent of societal cohesion, and that along with it, language also loses some of its meaning, as do rituals.

Against the backdrop of this disenchantment and the problems that arise along with it relative to the sociation of individuals, the coordination of action (individual and institutional), and the legitimation of conclusions; Habermas examines which contributions the social sciences, above all sociology, have made to the diagnosis and solution of these problems.

SYSTEM AS EXTERNAL ASPECT (Parsons)

Habermas sees Parsons's significance in that he recognized the necessity of connecting action theory to system theory. However, Habermas criticizes the fact that Parsons's approach fails before it achieves the coherent formulation of a theory. The introduction of system theory into sociology entails that acting individuals (and institutions) are viewed as systems oriented toward survival and optimizing their circumstances relative to the environment in which they find themselves. In order to fulfill this function, systems must not only process information external to the system, they must also be able to put themselves in the place of the other systems (how would I act if I were in his shoes?). On this basis, the environment becomes predictable for me, just as my behavior becomes predictable for others. This reciprocity raises the reliability of the expected resulting action. In his analysis, Parsons uses the LIGA Model (latency, integration, goal attainment, adaptation) that he designed himself.

Through countless modifications and extensions of this model, Parsons believes he has grasped all aspects of action, and in so doing, solved the problems of action coordination, the integration of individual and collective action goals and normative consenses. On the other hand, Habermas concludes that Parsons examines and characterizes action only from an "externalist" perspective. The perspective of the actor himself, the "meaning" that he ties to it, is ignored. Only the externally manifest aspect of the action can be grasped by this theory. Parsons's sociology is a theory of society and action without a subject and without a consciousness.

To the degree that the world is "behavioristic" and people orient their action according to expected rewards and punishments (of a material and normative type) Parsons's theory is a very good explanatory model. The fact, however, that this theory is seen as a key that fits in the lock that is society, so to speak, which presupposes the functioning of the lock itself, shows its limited explanatory potential. Habermas treats this deficiency on the basis of the theories of George Herbert Mead and ethnomethodology.

SYMBOLIC INTERACTION (Mead)

At the heart of Mead's symbolic interactionism is the assertion that humans, unlike animals, are not totally subject to the lures of their environment (and of their own needs). Humans can "steer" their reactions in that they determine to which attractions they will react, and to which they will respond by curbing or "diverting" their natural reaction. Moreover, humans also possess the chance to lend meaning to these lures. This potential comes with language ability.

Unlike a fight between two dogs (an example given by Mead), where every action in a predetermined pattern calls up a reaction, language (words interpreted as symbols) provides the interaction between people with an added dimension. Through language; purposes, expectations, and further reaching intentions can be communicated; one's own actions and those of others, as well, can be anticipated, and alternatives can be evaluated. The actual course of events then attains its true meaning from an "internalist" perspective, so to speak, in order not to show its actual reality. In this approach, rather than that of Parsons, Habermas sees the potential to explain and understand complicated coordination of activity and the following of rules by means of determining one's own behavior and judging the behavior of others. In Habermas's eyes, however, Mead's theory fails at the point where it limits coordinating and lending meaning to action and neglects the normative aspects.

ETHNOMETHODOLOGY

In ethnomethodology, above all in its development by Cicourel and Garfinkel, Habermas sees the chance not only to concretize Mead's approach, but also to bring together the perspective of the individual actor with that of the scientific approach. Habermas wants to illuminate the fact that the lens of the social sciences has (or better yet, must have) the same "rational internal structure" as the actors. Only then can we guarantee that all aspects of the actor may adequately be voiced in the research of the social sciences. Only then can a theory make a claim to the title "theory of communicative action." For this to happen, as we have seen, it is necessary that normative appropriateness, as well as truth and truthfulness claims, are recognized in their context in practice as well as in theory.

To be sure, in the existing sociological theories, Habermas sees approaches that are useful but too incomplete to be able to achieve a theory of action. Indeed, Parsons's theory touches on all aspects of action, but is ultimately content with an analysis from an "externalist" perspective; Mead's analysis from an "internalist" perspective neglects the normative; the ethnomethodologists push for a desirable blending of the perspectives of theory and practice; however, they use methods that are unclear and unproven. Habermas's own scientific-methodic approach stems from this critique in that he takes up the usable elements of antecedent attempts at theories. I cannot go into detail on Habermas's approach here. Rather, to conclude this study, I would like to briefly sketch how Habermas uses his method to achieve a diagnosis of the current situation.

HABERMAS'S TWO-LEVEL MODEL

That which was termed disenchantment above relative to cultural development with respect to Weber, Marx and Lukács, can be called reification for the dimensions of human experience and human action. Reification is the reduction of an action, which only achieves validity through providing meaning and normative justification, to its purposive rational element.

Through the development of our society into a system in which effectiveness and utility have become the only measures for the justification of actions, what we consider to be progress threatens to turn into just the opposite.

> Via the media of money and power, the subsystems of the economy and the state are differentiated out of an institutional complex set within the horizon of the lifeworld; formally organized domains of action emerge that—in the final analysis—are no longer

integrated through the mechanism of mutual understanding, that sheer off from lifeworld contexts and congeal into a kind of norm-free sociality.[14]

Habermas does not deny that differentiation of the quite distinct dimensions of action—goal oriented action, normative action and authenticity—offers evolutionary advantages. In every field the best methods can be sought to solve certain problems without burdening oneself with "irrelevant" issues.

The corresponding development of institutions in the broadest sense of the word, such as the administration of justice, police, social work, politics, economy and art, offers unprecedented opportunities for exploitation. In contrast to this, however, stands the deterioration of the lifeworld: the understanding reached between people that springs from their everyday interaction and deals with the distinctions between "good" and "evil" and with the meaning of that which one holds for "true" or "untrue," for "real" and "unreal."

The systems of the administration of justice, the economy and politics develop their own laws, and as Habermas sees it, they distanced themselves long ago from the purpose for which they were called into existence.

> Organizations gain autonomy through a *neutralizing demarcation from the symbolic structures of the lifeworld;* they become peculiarly *indifferent* to culture, society, and personality.[15]

They are parasites of the lifeworld in that they only meet the criterion of the means/ends rationality. From the lifeworld perspective, this process appears to be one of gaining autonomy. The rationality of the lifeworld, however, includes the much more important dimensions of normative legitimation and truthfulness. Traditional forms of human solidarity are destroyed through the increasing dominance of the systems (which Habermas discusses under the rubric "colonization"); at the same time, "cultural rationalization" threatens "to impoverish the lifeworld which has lost the value of the substance of its tradition."[16] Whereas economic exploitation and ideological deception were responsible for the alienation earlier on, now the source from which the power of resistance may be drawn is submerged. Total "externalist" control over that which can really only exist on the basis of an achieved understanding moves in and attacks the stubborn structures of the lifeworld.

Habermas couples this process to the "delinguistification" of law and economy through power and money. The delinguistified bureaucracy intervenes very subversively in socially integrated life circumstances, yet it can only exist—and this is what is both paradoxical but yet offers hope—as long as there is still communication. Here Habermas turns against the pessimism of the critical theory of Adorno and Horkheimer from *The Dialectic of Enlightenment*, in which the irreversible decline of our culture is outlined.

"Success" and "trouble free functioning" cannot unlimitedly legitimate themselves, or each question that is made of them. The instrumentalization of reason, as the one-sided emphasis of means/ends rationality is philosophically termed, cannot be taken further ad infinitum. To summarize in a practical, political way: the individual cannot be bound in every respect to society by system integration (reward-punishment); moreover, objectifying research in the social sciences can make statements about human beings that are only very limitedly "true." Ultimately, normative legitimation in politics is essential. Speaking scientifically, social processes cannot be completely objectified if we want to hold on to a sweeping claim to being able to understand and explain human behavior.

With the help of his two-level model of system and lifeworld, Habermas attempts to confront a total pessimism. The development of society has taken on a threatening character; however, there are still reserves in the lifeworld that could yet allow for the domination of this historic process once again. In spite of the great difference in this respect between Habermas on the one side and Horkheimer and Adorno on the other, Habermas em-

phasizes the concurrence of his program for research in the social sciences with that of traditional critical theory from the days
of the *Zeitschrift für Sozialforschung* [Journal of Social Research].
As it did then, research today must focus on these issues: the forms
of integration (individual-society) in the modern system, the model
of education, the mass media, the forms of protest and suppressed
protest, art, and finally, the critique of science.

Habermas is modest enough to leave it at simply identifying
these fields and to allow further, more substantive questions to
be answered in the respective fields. But the claim with which
he approaches the basis and the method of social-scientific
research is comprehensive enough and no less fundamental than
his political criticism of the doings and dealings of our political
system. In both respects, *The Theory of Communicative Action*
is a great book.

DETLEF HORSTER/
WILLEM VAN REIJEN
INTERVIEW WITH
JÜRGEN HABERMAS

(This interview took place on March 23, 1979 in Starnberg, Germany. This reprinted version appears with the kind approval of Intermediair (Amsterdam), where it was first published in June of 1979.)

Question: Mr. Habermas, you were sixteen years old at the end of the war, and barely four years old when the Nazis seized power. Your socialization essentially took place during the fascist rule. What influence has that had on your political development?

Habermas: I wouldn't want to say too terribly much about my youth. One does a real retrospective like that at seventy, not at fifty. I grew up in Gummersbach, in a small town environment. My father was head of the Chamber of Industry and Commerce there. My grandfather was the Director of the Seminary and Pastor. The political climate at home was probably nothing unusual for that period, specifically, characterized by a middle class conformity to a political environment with which one did not completely identify, but which one also did not criticize. Rather, it was the events of the year 1945 that set my political motives. At that time my personal life rhythm and the great historical events of the time coincided. I was fifteen years old. There were reports on the radio about the Nuremberg trials, and in the movie theaters they showed the first documentary films, the films about the concentration camps that we are seeing again today. I am sure that out of these experiences, motivations developed that determined the further course of my thinking.

Weren't your parents shocked then? Today, a film like Holocaust has the same effect on both young and old alike. How can it be explained that the earlier films you spoke about did not trigger any reaction, since most people obviously did not digest their experiences from that time?

The reaction to the earlier films and to *Holocaust* are two different things. I can only suppose that the enormous effect of Holocaust in part rests on the fact that here in the family setting, where the television is located, the younger generation asked their parents about the events of that time. We did not do that. I believe that at that time, we did not have the objectiveness to convert our own shock into a frontal confrontation within the family. I was still in the Hitler Youth and was on the Siegfried Line at fifteen. Our situation was dramatically different from that of the youth today. Our own history was suddenly bathed in a light that made all substantial aspects of it appear very different. We saw suddenly that it was a politically criminal system in which we had lived. I never had imagined that.

Does this mean that you never perceived what was happening to the Jews then; that you did not take the propaganda at its word?

In 1939 I was ten years old, and so I had no chance to get an especially positive picture. But naturally at that time there was the impression of a normality, which afterward turned out to be an illusion. We suddenly saw that our leaders were criminals; that has quite a different quality to it.

Against the backdrop of this moral distress, from the beginning, then, did you have a positive image of the society in which you lived and which eventually developed into the Federal Republic of Germany?

To begin with, 1945 represented a liberation, both historical and personal. Moreover, in my memory, it was beautiful weather. I found it all to be beautiful in a naive, intuitive way. Then I was bombarded with many impressions. I devoured the first books that were to be had in the newspaper press and those from the Marxist-Leninist book store. The first great political disappointments came with the formation of the government in 1949.

Why were you disappointed?

At that time I began to attend college, in Göttingen. My first political disappointments were the election meetings for the first parliament in Göttingen. I heard all kinds of people, among them Mr. Seebohm, who belonged to the German Peoples' Party. The party convention was decorated with black, white and red flags and was closed with the German national anthem. I fled absolutely full of emotion; I simply could not stand it. And this man was then elected Minister of Transportation. I thought, this simply cannot be possible that someone who embodies this continuity could sit in the first cabinet. But the real political problem was the rearmament. Heinemann (also a Minister in the first cabinet) was against it. I myself had very neutral views at that time. The experience of the war had made me a pacifist. Heinemann's resignation hit me hard.

Was that a very mixed situation for you then, on the one hand the National Socialist element, on the other hand hope for the realization of democratic civil rights and liberties? For some— Abendroth for example—the issue was clear: restoration of capitalism.

No, nothing at all was clear. I was nineteen, at that age one is still very immature. During my study, between 1949 and 1954, what was politically dominant for me was the very strong moral reaction to the Nazi period, and also the fear that a real break with the Nazi past had not taken place. At that time I thought what one can say today—not without some criticism: if only at least a spontaneous house cleaning had taken place, some explosive act that could then also have been the beginning for the formation of a political identity. After such an eruption, one at least would have known what one could no longer relapse into. There simply was no struggle. I believe that it makes a difference if one says this in retrospect or prospectively.

Why was it that the German people had no chance to form a political identity for themselves?

My concrete opinion is this: both before and during the invasion of the Allies, there was no spontaneous resistance and no clashes. Nobody took a risk so that the whole mess would finally end. I myself am a product of the "re-education," and I hope, not a very bad one. I mean to say that we learned then that the bourgeois constitutional state in its French or American or English character is a historic achievement. There is an important biographical difference between those who experienced what a half-hearted bourgeois republic like the Weimar Republic can lead to, and those who formed their political consciousness later on.

And the Republic after 1949 appeared to you to be more stable?

Naturally, for me, this state was a real chance.

But you were negatively impressed in many respects, as you just said?

I had no unbroken relationship with any party. Certainly not with the CDU [Christain-Democratic Union]. Antifascists founded this party right after 1945. But then I saw who joined it; in a small town, you know right away what is going on. And the Social Democrats; at first that was difficult for a middle class kid. Today it is unimaginable for the middle classes what that signified in terms of the social democracy of the Weimar Period that arose there again. And secondly, they had the Schumacher issue. He came out of a concentration camp with the complex: "We left the question of our nation to the Nazis in 1933." He met with a completely dissonant response with that kind of a program. The idea that we should be nationalists at a time like that was absurd to us. It was all the same to me whether Saarland is German or not. You must take into account this limited perspective that one had, educated at a university that in essence was unbroken in its continuity since the 1920s. All of the professors that were significant for me had been professors before 1933, and it stayed that way—with one exception, Professor Litt. In many subjects (philosophy, history, German studies, psychology) Göttingen was an apolitical and almost ethnocentric German university with a consciousness that was legitimate in 1910, when great scientific achievements were being made at German universities. In philosophy, for example, at that time in Bonn, Anglo-Saxon currents, even more so the analytical philosophy that was created by German emigrants, not to mention something like critical theory, were all simply nonexistent.

But in 1954, you still wrote a dissertation in the traditional sense. Were you able to free yourself from this tradition very quickly?

Until the appearance of the Heideggerian *Introduction to Metaphysics*, my political and my philosophical confessions, if you will, were two completely different things; that was in 1953. They were two universes that hardly touched. Then I saw that Heidegger, in whose philosophy I had lived, held this lecture in 1935 and published it without a single word of explanation. That was what really shocked me. I then wrote my first article in the *Frankfurter Allgemeine Zeitung* about that. I was naive, and I thought, how can one of our greatest philosophers do something like that? Naturally, one might have known all that much earlier, but I did not grow up like that. Also, around the same time, I read Lukács's *History and Class Consciousness*, which excited me very much.

How did you manage to come across History and Class Consciousness *at that time?*

Lukács was in the seminar library, which was relatively small; I felt at home there; I lived there. I knew every book there.

Through Löwith then I came across the young Marx. That caused me to write the introduction about the Young Hegelians for my dissertation—I added it after I had finished the dissertation, and it's probably quite obvious. I believe that I also came across Lukács in this context. I thought, what a shame that one cannot revive these motives in a systematic way. I was on the one side fascinated, and on the other side I knew that one can not do things like that anymore.
Politically that moved me very much. Then all the memories came back: I knew Marx from this book store in Gummersbach, but I had forgotten about him in the meantime. I had the feeling that it would be good if one could treat him in such a way that a systematic argument could be developed, but I realized with a certain sadness that one couldn't do that with Lukács. And then, if I may make a small jump, in 1955 I read *Dialectic of Enlightenment* by Horkheimer and Adorno. What immediately fascinated me about the both of them was that Marx was not treated critically, which they did not do, but rather used him constructively. That one could systematically make use of the Marxist tradition, that was a great discovery for me. Here were people that were

not writing a historic book about Aristotle, Kant or Hegel, but rather were establishing a theory about the dialectic development of modern society and in so doing, they conceived of it all from the Marxist tradition. For me, that was outrageous; I was prepared for it, however, by my study of Lukács. It was at that point that philosophical and political things began to touch one another for the first time.

Then you wrote The Structural Transformation of the Public Sphere?

Then I first studied empirical social research, then I wrote *Student und Politik*, then finally *The Structural Transformation of the Public Sphere.*

Your book on the public sphere was very disillusioning for the belief in democracy of the younger generation. At least it turned my political orientation completely upside down. For me, the only alternative left then was the Socialist German Student Alliance (SDS). Did you intend to have an effect like that?

I always had strong academic leanings. And naturally, I wrote *Transformation* above all to become clear myself about the dark sides and mistakes of our political system, the advantages of which I never doubted. At that time, a very strong restorative atmosphere prevailed, both socially and politically, an atmosphere that was so marked, I was completely shocked the first time my friend Apel called me a neo-Marxist. But then I realized that he was right. Today I set great store in being as a Marxist.

So you must also view *The Structural Transformation of the Public Sphere* against this setting. Behind it was the thought: How can one make clear to oneself what is somehow wrong about this political system, in spite of the Law, relative to political intentions. When the SDS was banned from the SDP, I was one of the three or four professors that founded the Socialist Alliance together with Abendroth. It was kind of an older man's version of the SDS. I cannot say that I wrote the book to inspire people to join the SDS. I wrote the book to make clear to myself and others that weaknesses exist in the political system of the Federal Republic that may become dangerous.

I would like to pose as a question a quote by Marx, which says that the limitations of the system lie in the system itself. Do you see this in the same way, that something perhaps is not right with the fundamental liberal values themselves? That (this) self-destruction is unavoidable? To put it differently: Where do you get your optimism?

Optimism? One must make a distinction here. It is true that I do not share the basic assumptions of critical theory as they were formed at the beginning of the 1940s. The assumption is that instrumental reason has come so far to its position of dominance that there is no longer any path leading out of this totally blinding context, in which only small flashes of insight are possible that may hit isolated individuals. Up to today I have been irritated by a contradiction. On the one hand our social system, certainly the capitalist social system in general but the Federal Republic perhaps in a special way, is relatively stable, and not just economically. It guarantees not only a relatively conflict-free mode of co-existence, but it also has institutionalized political freedoms that first must be seen and affirmed from a historical perspective. But on the other hand, this society creates many symptoms that make me afraid. On an intuitive level, I am actually convinced that something very deep within this system has been structured wrongly. This irritates me, it is also a motivation for my theoretical efforts, and perhaps for a certain oscillation. I am not Marxist in the sense that I take Marxism almost as a patent. But yet Marxism gave me the impetus and the analytical means to investigate how the relationship of democracy and capitalism developed.

But this means then that you really are convinced that exist-ing power structures can also be broken by means of a theoreti-cal analysis.

Yes, I firmly believe that the left in general, and the Marxists in particular, can retain one advantage over all other political pow-ers, and it is the belief that we can convey theoretical analyses with a middle or long-term perspective in the politics of every-day life. We should not relinquish this legacy. On the other hand, I also believe that we have fewer convincing analyses than ever before. This is probably also a reason why at times I clashed with the students more than perhaps politically necessary. What I ab-solutely misunderstood were dogmatisms that manifested them-selves even with anarchical students. They were probably non-dogmatic in the ways in which they lived and interacted. . .

But your critique at that time was of a different point; name-ly, that theoretical considerations were supposed to be tested direct-ly in actual practice by the SDS in such a spontaneous way. Cer-tain criticisms of the SDS—and here I am certainly in unison with the critics of that time—have proven to be right, as we can see today; for example, the criticism of their delusion that they had made so much progress with society that they could raise the red flag at a seminar. But was it right at that time to criticize in this way? Oskar Negt reproached you for a lack of solidarity demon-strated by your behavior. Lack of solidarity in that you inspired the student revolt on the one hand, but on the other hand dis-tanced yourself from it and criticized it from the outside. Is it pos-sible that at that time, a discourse about social problems was neces-sary, instead of criticism with clinical terms? Could you not as-sume that if you act in such a way, there will be a distance that cannot be bridged?

I want to question a premise: specifically, that I positioned myself outside of the student movement. I have never viewed it in that way, and it certainly never was intended.

Did you not want to consider your involvement finished with the remarks you made?

No. At that time the disagreement had not even really begun when I made this somewhat out of place remark about leftist fascism. No, I did not at all make a complete break.

I criticized publicly on two occasions. The first time was after the Benno Ohnesorg demonstration in Hannover. I later published my opinions in 1969 in *Protestbewegung und Hochschulreform*. I still believe the substance of my statement was right, but I should have expressed it with other words. The second time was at Pentecost, right after the passing of the emergency laws. The SDS had planned a congress of high school and college students. The students came from all over the Federal Republic. A march was planned from the opera house to the university, which was manned by police. I thought that was irresponsible; there was criticism even among the participants. You can read about these things. It was the time of the French May, and the students really thought the revolution had come. That was the context of the whole affair.

Relative to the content, I agree with you, but the way in which . . .

I know that I psychologized, but for each sentence I could give you a past history of what had brought me to say what I did. You have to look at how concrete it all was. And everybody realized it at that time. Today we read about it and see it very differently. And then it was an *internal* critique of the method of the protest movement. You ask me about my desolidarity. It is true that I did not grow up in an organization; in which one would I have? For that reason perhaps I reacted a touch too much in the direction of a middle class intellectual. On the other hand, the illusion of the students that they were, so to speak, living the continuance of the tradition of the workers' movement was equally wrong. In the wake of it all, even looking back, I still do not believe that I would have had a chance if I had not been so outspoken.

Did that not shake your faith in this kind of political confrontation? Because you brought no influence to bear on the events?

Actually, it was my wish to bring my influence to bear. The leadership of the SDS spoke to me in no uncertain terms and with no reservations, but that had passed by the middle of 1967. And my attempt to exert an influence had to take this form. It was at that point that the image appeared that Habermas was really distancing himself from the protest movement. Even the introduction to *Protestbewegung und Hochschulreform* demonstrated a clear identification with the goals of the protest movement.

At the time Klaus Meschkat charged that you had a strange relation to reality because you made no mention in your Frankfurt speech that there had been demonstrations throughout the entire Federal Republic of Germany and that the French May had also occurred. Looking back, would you not admit that there was consciously an awful lot more going on than we could see at that time? The student movement had reached a point of no return.

But that is all in my theses. Look at the last thesis. It expresses real optimism with respect to the protest movements.

Do you still view the protest movement as extremely important for the development of the Federal Republic?

In the normative area, in the views, in the cultural value system, there was a break.

But today, one would rather see the opposite, that students today are more than ever prepared to submit themselves to all kinds of restrictive conditions.

No, there are studies that even compare internationally and show that the value system of the entire population has changed. What Ms. Noelle-Neumann describes as a proletarization of the middle class values could also be described in a more adequate way. A distancing from the value orientations that determined the political culture of the 1950s is reflected in this phenomenon. Instrumentalist, privatist, competitively determined, career oriented, familial value syndromes have begun to flounder in parts of the population, as the shift from the "old" to the "new politics" shows.

But is it not the case that precisely where such attitudes are changed, no political change is effected? To be sure, changes in attitudes can be perceived, but people that change their attitudes fall out of the political system and become systematically underprivileged.

As a complementary question, I want to ask you: If we no longer have the values of the 1950s, what do we have in their place?

To begin with, we can see a lot of traces of the protest movement. Changes in family structure, changes in the way in which we raise our young are bolder. In part, the protest movement is already a product of changed socialization forms. We must also put this in a broader perspective. But first off, we are in agreement that the protest movement was effective in bringing about cultural re-orientations. Now you ask which political consequences such changes have? Should one not be rather skeptical here? As it is, you are pushing me into the false role of an optimist. As I see it at the moment, new political potentials form that can be of serious, dysfunctional consequences and can exercise pressure for a veto.

This pressure for a veto could usher in a re-organization of the party system in the long term, and I do not necessarily mean that in the way in which Strauss means it. But I am leery of making specific prognoses. We are dealing here with historic trends that are hard to diagnose. I think that there is a lot of room for alternative developments in which the party system can react to new challenges. If there ever were a real government of the right that was rigorous about developing a new economic policy in the sense of Milton Friedman, that would mean a gradual elimination of the social-welfare state. That in turn could lead to a revitalization of traditional class struggles. But I assume that this government also would be clever enough to calculate such risks.

I share your view that we will not very quickly come to an elimination of the social-welfare state. On the other hand, what still affected me, and I do not want to attach too much importance to an isolated event, was this discussion in Holland with Helmut Kohl. The agitation was tremendous. The Germans were clearly more shocked, and certainly Kohl as well, that a particular principle of discussion had been violated, more so than that touchy subjects were being discussed. Specifically, that in a television interview, the moderator and Kohl did not succeed in maintaining the upper hand. The Dutch said, "We determine what is an answer and what is not." That shocked the German viewers. I ask myself if the trend to forming an educated public is not stronger in Germany than in Holland. If what we saw on such a broadcast is not exemplary.

I did not see that broadcast. But I assume that it is a symptom of corporate limitations on a functioning middle class pluralism. And in my experience, the symptoms of that are stronger in the Federal Republic than in the United States or England. But it is not as if I only see a clear blue sky over me. On the contrary, after the kidnapping of Schleyer, the politicians, the media, the press with few exceptions, and not just the papers to the right of the *Frankfurter Allgemeine Zeitung*, tore down the barriers of political culture that were so painstakingly erected in the first two decades after the war. In those first two decades, an official opinion was forced on the German public that was substantially more liberal than the composite attitude of the people. These healthy controls were destroyed, suddenly people demanded that Böll emigrate, one had to consider the possibility that hostages could be shot, etc. Such feelings do exist, naturally, but to express them had not been possible up to that point. Then in addition to that, there were bureaucratically decreed stirs of emotion, the trend to make citizens into auxiliary police, etc. I remember a press conference at which the association Freiheit der Wissenschaft [Freedom in Science] made public the names of professors, of colleagues that allegedly belonged to the sympathizers. I believe that the high degree of social integration in the Federal Republic is deceptive, and it has a drawback: strongly suppressed emotions and attitudes that bubble up to the surface in extreme situations. Or in any case, whenever one of the large parties pushes it. If the CDU had not gone along with it, we never would have had that German Autumn.

At that time you sounded the attack in your essay in the Spiegel. *Many people were happy that you again took part in the public political discussion. But then you did not take part in the Russell tribunal.*

I miscalculated the effect the first Russell tribunal would have. I was afraid that afterward the whole discussion about professional bans would be pushed off into illegality. I thought that the inappropriate institutional parameters of the Russell tribunal for the Federal Republic had the effect of discrediting the issue to such an extent that we would never get anywhere with it afterward. At that time I thought—and you may say this is typical of an intellectual—that ten or twenty people would be brought together in Harheim to counter the expected publicistic effect. People who could then say, "we did not support the Russell tribunal, but what happened there really is a scandal." But I never got this group together. Moreover, it should have been left at only the first Russell tribunal, because the second Russell tribunal had only a single "case," and that was one particular law affecting journalists. What was discussed there were factual cases of censure, which is not worse in the Federal Republic than in any other western country.

The Buback Affair and students that neglect to deal with Marx in their theses because they want to become teachers—is all of this not somehow typical for the situation in the Federal Republic?

It certainly is!

All the things that are done to suppress the formation of educated opinions. . .

Well, any liberal would answer you, and I hope rightfully so, that somehow we endured the situation. Mr. Nixon had to be removed first. Ultimately, a democracy preserves itself not with the products that it allows, but rather in the way in which it deals with them.

But precisely in this respect we must focus on a certain issue: this reverse in faith that was put before the teachers in Lower Saxony. . .

What Pestel did is a scandal, a throwback to the McCarthy Era and I would also like to add that the fact that most of the professors who were requested to, actually did sign; that is a scandal, too.

But it is not only a question for the Federal Republic, but rather also a question for the smaller countries all around us. The Federal Republic has such strong economic power. That does have an effect on the political structure of neighboring countries.

I am no fan of a united Europe, nor was I when it was popular, either, but one must be happy about the growing integration of the European countries.

. . . about the confrontation with systems that attach more importance to political education and forming an educated political opinion. . .

. . . also in a framework in which there is France and England, and above all, the southern European countries with strong communist parties.

Even in the Federal Republic, a stronger Euro-communist party could be a liberalizing factor in some respects. Many things would then become normalized. In this country, for example, one does not become Director of the Max Planck Institute or professor or whatever if he is a Marxist. As long as that is the case, the fundamental nature of the political culture is not liberal.

One last question about the political sphere: where do you see your personal future political activity?

Whether I can still have a certain effect for the political consciousness of the left in the Federal Republic, I do not know. Naturally that is not to say that one does not have the usual academic influence, for example, on college students.

And your theoretical influence? And the target group, young academics?

You can call it that. But what is a young academic? There is something to the conservative uproar about the "purveyors of meaning" to the degree that the normative horizon of our society has become more sensitive. It is perhaps not just an illusion on the part of an old fan of the Enlightenment with nonsense from the 18th century when I say that we can attempt argumentation situations through books. If necessary, one can filter in through articles in the daily press, which, naturally, no one creates on purpose, but which are important for interpretations. What I am going to say now will sound very old-fashioned. If one can illuminate a diffuse situation that nobody has described so readily, that has to touch the understanding, even the self-understanding, of broader social groups. That simply is tied to the exceptionally effective media system that we have. But at the moment, I see no "target group." We spoke briefly about these new political potentials. It would be my idea to contribute to the interpretation of conflicts that arise on the margins of highly adjudicated, bureaucratic life spheres, of life spheres ploughed up by technology. Whoever correctly interprets an unclear situation only has the success that one has when one comes even a small bit closer to the truth; he may even influence something that is already clear, that ultimately influences political orientations. On the other hand, God knows I do not share the instrumentalist idea that is widespread among the literati of the trend change that one could trim the objective spirit to the left or the right by means of ideology planning, and linguistic politics.

I have only one practical problem, namely conveying to students the problems that are treated in Reconstruction of Historic Materialism. *Students slowly despair because of the enormous synthesis of different theories, and they say, "Well, if we had to fulfill all the sociological prerequisites and then the evolution-theoretical, etc. . . .*

Yes, right, but I also see the problem in a different way. I understand the practical difficulties in conveying your theory. But the difficulties are to be found in the issue itself. Bloch always said: I cannot write about the subject in a more simple way because the subject itself is not simple. This is no problem for dogmatic Marxism, they simply shake a social analysis out of their sleeve. However, with the blunt instruments of Marxist theory, for exam-

ple, with the "Tendentious Case of the Profit Rate," one cannot explain, or at least, one cannot convincingly explain the crisis here. But the object of our analysis, "society," is itself unwieldy. This is shown as well by other sociological theories that cast about for opportunities to combine with yet other sociological theories in the hope of getting a better handle on the object of their analysis. Naturally, I would admit that it is a problem for students to know all theories. But one cannot get around a view of the object without confronting it directly, or I would have to sell my social analysis short. I see nothing else in your theoretical approaches, Mr. Habermas.

I think what you just said is very nice. Only I must say that Mr. van Reijen is right about one thing: what is reflected in the difficulties of my texts are certainly also my own uncertainties. There is no question about that.

You just said that you think what I said was very nice. Do you only think it is nice, or would you also say it is the way in which you see the matter yourself.

Yes.

If you are in agreement with that, I would like to proceed to the following question. Your theory is the synthesis of different theories with differing paradigms; just to name a few: action theory, philosophy of language, Marxist theory, evolution theory. The discussions of the last sociologists' gathering had to do with the problem of the possibility of theory comparison and synthesis. Which criteria do you have for your syntheses? Can theories with such different paradigms even be synthesized?

I see that somewhat differently. If you ask me if one can "marry" behavior theory, i.e. the learning theory small group research as it was developed in the U.S. in the 1950s, with one that begins with action theory, be it Parsons or be it Marxist sociology, I would say: no. The basic concepts are mutually exclusive. In one case the sphere of objects is conceptualized by eliminating the basic concept of meaning, in another case, intentional action, communicative action or value oriented action are taken up as the basic concept. These are clear alternatives. I would never try to integrate such theoretical approaches. On the other hand, I do not at all believe that such a large number of paradigms exists. This is rather an artificial product of scientific rhetoric unintentionally inspired by Kuhn.

In the theoretical history of sociology, to the extent that it could even make a societal-theoretical claim, from Marx, Durkheim, Weber to Parsons and whomever, the same problem always existed on the level of basic concepts: how do we link system and action paradigms, or system and lifeworld paradigms? Marx eliminated the problem entirely by adapting the Hegelian basic concepts, since the Hegelian basic concept is at the same time neutral with respect to this differentiation. For this reason, Marx was also able to develop a theory on the value of work that serves to translate the functionalist analysis of the process of exploitation, or system analyses, into analyses that refer to class conflicts and acting subjects and groups. Actually I do not think it is possible to salvage the theory of the value of work. Moreover, that is one of the reasons why many people do not consider me a Marxist. But certainly there must be a systematic equivalent.

In the course of his development, Parsons transferred the theory of action into systems theory, but not without some fragments left over. This is clear in the status of the so-called "general frame of action" which advanced to the general action system. My assertion is that the problem exists in relating the two paradigms to each other not simply in a rhetorical way, but rather to refer them to each other in a satisfactory way. Only then can we systematically take up the basic questions of Marx. Speaking casually, that is the question of how capitalist development, which must be systematically analyzed, has its effects on the structures of the lifeworld (of those classes affected most directly, now basically the entire population). The dialectic of reified and living work should explain how we came to the destruction of the traditional life forms in the social classes out of which the proletariat developed. It had to do with the declaration of the proletarization of life forms. For Marx, that was more of a practical stimulus, and in that way we can relate his thesis to our current situation.

Our problems are still how this capitalist economic system, which does not grow so poorly, destroys life conditions which are so structured that they must be described in action theoretical categories. As soon as one interprets away the infrastructure of lifeworlds in a system-theoretic way, when one allows only social life spheres that can be systematically regulated on an analytic level, at that moment, one can no longer speak about sociated individuals; at best about Martians, about existences that are so defined that one can no longer recognize sociated individuals and their problems with this description.

Well, from the structuralist interpretation of Marx I could see that there is not such a big difference between systems theory and this interpretation of Marx. But can action theory be synthesized with Marxist theory just like that? As regards the actions of humans, action theory cannot cover what goes on in their consciousness. Thus, the mute compulsion of the situation falls through the analytic net.

I believe that what Marx was interested in was reaching by means of consciousness, objective life contexts through which the action orientations of subjects can then best be reconstructed when one understands that an idealism is built into the action-theoretical basic concept. In the serious action-theoretical approaches like the linguistic (Winch), or the phenomenological (Schütz), or the ethnomethodological (Garfinkel), society is basically defined as a lifeworld that is completely transparent. Instead, I would tend to see society as systemically stabilized action contexts of social-

ly integrated groups. Let me formulate this as a task: if we succeed in putting together system and action paradigms in the right
way, we may sue for the posing of Marxist questions, instead of
merely defining them away, as is done in both systems and action theory. Thus, the diversity of theoretic approaches that I attempt to integrate is not so large.

Precisely, there is still a problem that must be solved, name-
ly, relative to your emancipation theory. If I understood the argu-
ment of the ideal speech situation in a future society correctly,
that implies then the idealistic hope that whole social systems
change due to changes in single individuals, the communicative
actions of individual humans? . . . like Kuhn, you are haunted
by the paradigms.

There you have to look at the place value. First I need the
ideal speech situation in order to reconstruct the normative foundations of a critical theory. The theory communication that I have
in mind begins with a type of action oriented toward reaching
an understanding, in which those taking part orient themselves
according to criticizable validity claims. Whether an understanding
is reached is measured according to whether the validity claim
that is raised by ego is accepted by age, or not. In this context
I must show what it means to raise and vindicate validity claims,
i.e. the truth claim of an assertion. Now I believe that there are
precisely two validity claims that can only be vindicated argumen-
tatively. That leads me to a discourse theory about truth, and
thereby I return to the general pragmatic prerequisites of the ideal
speech situation.

We do not need to imagine the ideal speech situation as a
utopian pattern for an emancipated society. I am using it only
for the reconstruction of the concept of reason, that is, a concept
of communicative reason that I would like to introduce opposite
Adorno and Horkheimer's *Dialectic of Enlightenment*. With Horkheimer and Adorno, reason collapses to the "unreason" of mi-

mesis. The promise of reconciliation is lifted in mimetic forces. With Adorno, then, this leads to a negative dialectic, and that means "nowhere."

Then the identity point of view for you would not be acceptable? But the salvation of reason leads us to say that there will still be ruling forces even in a future society. An old problem with Schelling. If the rule of reason continues to exist, then rule over the objects will always remain, as well. In contrast, there is only one possible solution that was offered by Schelling: identity.

I believe that this belongs to the conceptual legacies that simply cannot see eye to eye. There is, if you will, just a bit of Kant in me. There is something that remains unreconciled to nature.

If we talk about reason, then we do not speak about decisions for value postulates, but rather we speak about unavoidable preconditions that are not at our disposition. The aspects of reason, which according to Max Weber are irreconcilably separated—cognitively instrumental, morally practical, aesthetically expressive—these three still form a differentiated concept of reason. Max Weber is wrong—I would say—when he thinks that the autonomous instances of reason are transformed into irrational ideologies that compete with one another. No, they remain instances of reason, and the big question is: How can we describe their context in a sufficiently precise way? What does this context of reason mean for the sociation of individuals that speak and work and, in that they do both, can do nothing other than reproduce their life with the help of precisely this three-stranded reason. I certainly do not believe—and Max Weber is right here—that we can take custody of the unity of reason, the context of the moments of reason on the level of cultural interpretation systems, thus, in the form of a religious world-view or a philosophy.

Moreover, speaking Marxist: abolition of philosophy. On the level of cultural interpretation systems, nothing fits together any

more. But in life circumstances and in the communicative everyday practice, the instances of reason are still connected, just in
a strangely altered way. This is also Marx's question: the destruction of precisely these reasonably structured life circumstances
by the ramifications of an economic-administrative system that,
viewed for itself, has reached a high level of system differentiation, but is still set up in such a way that it has destructive side
effects, and these are the problem. From the rationalization point
of view—as formulated by Weber—that which for me constitutes
the idea of socialism, is the possibility of overcoming the propen-
sity for one-sidedness of the rationalization process; one-sidedness
in the sense of the cognitive-instrumental aspects becoming
dominant, and everything else has been pushed through them
into the seemingly irrational. Everything else would be moved,
so to speak, to the correct place, not as if there had ever been
a phase in which they had not been in the correct place. Even
in socialism, one would have to live with an economic system
that operates just like a differentiated partial system, but which
does not develop this objective, penetratingly destructive force
that works behind our backs for communicatively structured life
circumstances.

What I would criticize about Marx is the following: he did
not see that with the capitalist system of production, not only was
a new, unpolitical form of class rule established, but also along
with it a new level of system differentiation—Luhmann would
say—with tremendous evolutionary advantages relative to the level of system differentiation that pre-bourgeois state organized societies attained. Such evolutionary advantages—if one would
choose to put it so—are not available. Marx thought if we would
smash the capital, then the economy would dissolve into a
lifeworld context under our control. Later, he saw the situation
somewhat more skeptically (separation of the sphere of necessity from the sphere of freedom).

Marx talked about neutral forces of productivity; I wonder if there are neutral increases in complexity or if this is the higher level of system differentiation reached in modernity only at the price of some form of class rule. If the latter is the case, there would only be regressive solutions for socialism. That makes the matter not necessarily more unattractive, but almost impossible. How should a situation look in which the population mass would be prepared to pay a substantial price for more humane forms of co-existence? But there are no *a priori* arguments for the pessimistic assumption that lies at the bottom of this question; for this reason, socialization is a project structured so that it is capable of self-correction, fallibilist, so to speak, and as essential today as ever.

NOTES

Chapter 1: Jürgen Habermas - Social Analyst and Combative Democrat

1. Jürgen Habermas, The Structural Transformation of the Public Sphere, transl. Thomas Burger, (Cambridge, MA: MIT Press, 1989), 142.
2. Ibid., 232.
3. Habermas, Technik und Wissenschaft als 'Ideologie', (Frankfurt am Main: Suhrkamp, 1968), 107.
4. Ibid., 62.
5. Ibid., 62-3.
6. Habermas, "Stumpf gewordene Waffen aus dem Arsenal der Gegenaufklärung: Brief an Sontheimer vom 19.9.1977," in Briefe zur Verteidigung der Republik, ed. Freimut Duve et al, (Reinbek/Hamburg: Rohwolt, 1977), 70.
7. Habermas, Knowledge and Human Interests, transl. Jeremy J. Shapiro, (Boston: Beacon Press, 1971), 42. Passage italicized in the original.
8. Habermas, Zur Rekonstruktion des Historischen Materialismus, (Frankfurt am Main: Suhrkamp, 1976), 162.
9. Habermas, Die neue Unübersichtlichkeit, (Frankfurt am Main: Suhrkamp, 1985), 215.
10. Albrecht Wellmer, Praktische Philosophie und Theorie der Gesellschaft: Zum Problem der normativen Grundlagen einer kritischen Sozialwissenschaft, (Konstanz: Universitätsverlag, 1979), 10.
11. Habermas, Vorstudien und Ergänzungen zur Theorie des kommunikativen Handelns, (Frankfurt am Main: Suhrkamp, 1984), 593.
12. Habermas, "Entgegnung", Kommunikatives Handeln, eds. Axel Honneth und Hans Joas, (Frankfurt am Main: Campus,1986), 332.
13. Ibid., 391.
14. Habermas, "Waffen", loc. cit. 71.

15. Ibid., 72.
16. Habermas, The Philosophical Discourse of Modernity, (Cambridge, MA: MIT Press, 1987), 43-4.
17. Ibid., 113.
18. Habermas, Unübersichtlichkeit, loc. cit. 141.
19. Ibid., 143.
20. Ibid., 161-2.
21. Habermas, Eine Art Schadensabwicklung, (Frankfurt am Main: Suhrkamp, 1987), 129.
22. Ibid., 131.
23. Ibid., 140.

Chapter 2: Habermas's Linguistic Philosophy

1. Herbert Schnädelbach, "Philosophie", Philosophie: Ein Grundkurs, eds. Ekkehard Martens and Schnädelbach, (Reinbek/Hamburg: Rohwolt, 1985), 59. On the subject of change in paradigm see the excellent work by Ernst Tugendhat, Vorlesungen zur Einführung in die sprachanalytische Philosophie, (Frankfurt am Main: Suhrkamp, 1976). Habermas also commented on this subject in his essay "Die Einheit der Vernunft in der Vielheit ihrer Stimmen" in Merkur 1 (1988): 1-14.
2. See Habermas's introductory lecture from 1965 "Erkenntnis und Interesse" in the book of the same name (Knowledge and Human Interests). Also, see Technik und Wissenschaft als 'Ideologie', loc. cit. especially p. 155.
3. Edmund Husserl, The Crisis of Eurppean Sciences and Transcendental Phenomenology, transl. David Carr, (Evanston, IL: Northwestern University Press, 1970), 104.
4. Habermas, Knowledge and Human Interests, n.p.
5. Husserl, 315-34.
6. Jürgen Habermas, The Theory of Communicative Action, vol. 2, (Boston: Beacon Press, 1984), 35.
7. Habermas, "Entgegnung", loc. cit. 332.
8. Habermas, letter to the author, 17 January 1986.
9. Husserl, loc. cit. 185-6.
10. Habermas, "Moral und Sittlichkeit" in Merkur 12 (1985): 1043. See also Habermas, "Entgegnung", loc. cit. 334.
11. George Herbert Mead, The Philosophy of the Present, ed. Arthur E. Murphy, (LaSalle, IL: Open Court Publishing Co., 1959): 184-190.
12. Husserl, loc. cit. 146-7.

13. Habermas, Vorstudien, loc. cit. 394-5; cf. also Habermas, "Entgegnung", loc. cit. 358-9.
14. Habermas, "Entgegnung", loc. cit. 356-7.
15. The diagram is made according to that in Habermas, Vorstudien, loc. cit. 405.
16. Habermas, "Entgegnung", loc. cit. 357.
17. Habermas, "Vorbereitende Bemerkungen zu einer Theorie der kommunikativen Kompetenz", Theorie der Gesellschaft oder Sozialtechnologie, Habermas and Niklas Luhmann, (Frankfurt am Main: Suhrkamp, 1971), 105; the entire passage is italicized in the original text.
18. See Habermas, Vorstudien, loc. cit. 406.
19. Ibid., 407.
20. Ibid., 395.
21. Ibid., 432; the entire passage is italicized in the original text.
22. Ibid., 433; the entire passage is italicized in the original text.
23. Ibid., 101-2.
24. Ibid., 103.
25. Ibid., 137.
26. Ibid., 138-9.
27. Ibid., 130-1.
28. Habermas, "Vorbereitende Bemerkungen", loc. cit. 117.
29. See Burkhard Tuschling, Die "offene" und die "abstrakte" Gesellschaft, (Berlin: Argument, 1978), 155.
30. Habermas, "Vorbereitende Bemerkungen", loc. cit. 131; some italics are added here.
31. Ibid., 134.
32. Ibid., 134-5.
33. Ibid., 136; some italics are added here.
34. Ibid., 137.
35. Habermas, Vorstudien, loc. cit. 177-8; for the derivation of the ideal speech situation see Habermas, "Vorbereitende Bemerkungen", loc. cit. 140.
36. Ibid., 162.
37. Ibid., 164.
38. Ibid., 170-1.
39. For this example, cf. ibid., 165.
40. Cf. ibid., 172-3.
41. Ibid., 171-2.
42. Ibid., 175.
43. Ibid., 176.
44. Ibid., 104.

45. Conversation between Jürgen Habermas, Axel Honneth, Eberhard Knödler-Bunte and Arno Widmann, "Dialektik und Rationalisierung", Ästhetik und Kommunikation, 45/46 (1981): 131.
46. Cf. ibid., 154.

III. Habermas's Reconstruction of Reason

1. Cf. R. Schottländer, "Nous als Terminus", Hermes 64 (1929): 229.
2. Cf. my volume on Kant that appears in this series (Zur Einführung), the section entitled "Das Deduktionskapitel".
3. Günther Patzig, "Platon", Klassiker des philosophischen Denkens, ed. Norbert Hoerster, vol. 1 (Munich: DTV, 1982), 51.
4. Aristotle, Nicomachean Ethics, Book 6, Chapter 13.
5. Kurt Flasch, introduction to Geschichte der Philosophie in Text und Darstellung, ed. R. Bubner, vol. 2, (Stuttgart: Reclam, 1982), 14.
6. Thomas von Kempen, Die Nachfolge Christi, Book 6, Chapter 18.2.
7. Karl-Heinz Volkmann-Schluck, Nicolaus Cusanus: Die Philosophie im Übergang vom Mittelalter zur Neuzeit, 2nd ed., (Frankfurt am Main: Klostermann, 1968), 179.
8. Cf. Willem van Reijen, "Freiheit und Moral in der Philosophie Descartes'", Zeitschrift für philosophische Forschung 1 (1975): 125-6.
9. Cf. both sections entitled "Zwischenbetrachtung" in my volume on Kant.
10. Habermas, Theory of Communicative Action, vol. 1, 392.
11. Habermas, "Die Einheit der Vernunft und die Vielheit ihrer Stimmen", Merkur 1 (1988): 12.
12. Habermas, Theory of Communicative Action, vol. 1, loc. cit. 58.
13. Cf. ibid., vol. 2, 10.
14. Cf. ibid., 15.
15. Ibid., 23.
16. Ibid., 86.
17. Ibid., 46.
18. Cf. ibid., 52.
19. Cf. ibid., 77-8.
20. Ibid., 82.
21. Ibid., 135.
22. Cf. ibid., 138.
23. Ibid., 127.
24. Ibid., 390.
25. Cf. ibid., 305 and 307. Habermas learned from Parsons how the media of money and power develop, cf. ibid., 264 and 280-1.

26. Ibid., 305.
27. Ibid., 325.
28. Cf. ibid., 303-4.
29. Ibid., 62.
30. Cf. ibid., 185.
31. Ibid., 275.
32. Ibid., 395.
33. Ibid., 397-8.
34. Cf. Ibid., 400.
35. Cf. Habermas, The Philosophical Discourse of Modernity, 16-8.
36. Ibid., 20.
37. Ibid., 41-2.
38. Ibid., 29.
39. Ibid., 297.
40. Ibid., 298.
41. Ibid., 297.
42. Habermas, "Moral und Sittlichkeit", Merkur 12 (1985): 1043.
43. Ibid., 1041.
44. Ibid.
45. Cf. Habermas, Moralbewutsein und kommunikatives Handeln, (Frankfurt am Main: Suhrkamp, 1983), 75-6.
46. Habermas, "Moral und Sittlichkeit", loc. cit. 1046.
47. See Karl-Otto Apel, Transformation der Philosophie, vol. 2, (Frankfurt am Main: Suhrkamp, 1973), 400.
48. Habermas, "Moral und Sittlichkeit", loc. cit. 1042-3.
49. Ibid., 1046.
50. Cf. ibid., 1042.
51. Ibid., 1049-50.
52. Ibid., 1052.

Willem van Reijen:
The Erosion of Western Culture

Without exception the notes in this chapter refer to Habermas's Theory of Communicative Action, (Boston: Beacon Press, 1984); only volume and page numbers are given.

1. Vol. 1, xl.
2. Cf. ibid., 139.
3. Vol. 2, 368.
4. Ibid., 369.
5. Ibid., 367.
6. Vol. 1, 340.
7. Ibid., 16.
8. Ibid., 10.
9. Ibid., 75.
10. Ibid., 140.
11. Ibid., 164.
12. Ibid., 273.
13. Ibid., 342.
14. Vol. 2, 307.
15. Ibid.
16. n.p.

SELECTED BIBLIOGRAPHY

Books by Habermas in English

Toward a Rational Society: Student Protest,Science and Politics, (Boston, 1970)
Knowledge and Human Interests (Boston, 1971)
Theory and Practice (Boston, 1973)
Legitimation Crisis (Boston, 1975)
Communication and the Evolution of Society (Boston, 1979)
Philosophical - Political Profile (Cambridge, 1984)
The Theory of Communicative Action, vol 1: *Reason and the Rationalization of Society,* (Boston, 1984)
The Theory of Communicative Action, vol 2: *Lifeworld and System: A Critique of Functionalist Reason* (Boston, 1987)
The Philosophical Discourse of Modernity, Twelve Lecture (Cambridge, 1987)
On the Logic of the Social Science (Cambridge, 1988)
Moral Consciousness and Communicative Action (Cambridge, 1989)
The Structural Transformation of the Public Sphere (Cambridge, 1989)

Anthology

Seidman, Steve (ed.) *Jürgen Habermas on Society and Politics: A Reader* (Boston, 1989)

Some Critical Works on Habermas

Brand, Arie: *The Force of Reason: An Introduction to the Work of Jürgen Habermas* (London, 1989)
Guess, Raymond: *The Idea of Critical Theory. Habermas and the Frankfurt School* (Cambridge, 1981)

Ingram, David: *Habermas and the Dialectic of Reason*
(New Haven, 1987)
McCarthy, Thomas: *The Critical Theory of Jürgen Habermas*
(Cambridge 1978)
White, Stephen: *The Recent Work of Jürgen Habermas. Reason, justice and modernity* (Cambridge, 1988)

The following journals should also be consulted:

New German Critique
Philosophy & Social Criticism
Praxis International

CHRONOLOGICAL TABLE

1929   Born on June 18 in Düsseldorf; grows up in Gummersbach
1949   Abitur and subsequent study of philosophy, history, psychology
        and German literature in Göttingen, Zürich and Bonn
1954   Doctorate in Bonn: *"The Absolute and the History of the Con-
        tradictory Nature of Schelling's Thought"*; Habermas identifies
        Erich Rothacker, Oskar Becker, Nicolai Hartmann, Wilhelm
        Keller, Theodor Litt, Johannes Thyssen and Hermann Wein as his
        teachers of philosophy
1956   Assistant at the Frankfurt Institute for Social Research
1961   Wrote *Student und Politik* together with Ludwig von Friedeburg,
        Christoph Oehler and Friedrich Weltz
1962   Postdoctorate work with Wolfgang Abendroth in Marburg with
        the writing *Structural Transformation of the Public Sphere*; before
        this work has concluded, Habermas becomes professor of
        philosophy in Heidelberg
1963   *Theorie und Praxis*
1964   Professor of philosophy and sociology in Frankfurt am Main
1968   *Knowledge and Human Interests, Technik und Wissenschaft als
        'Ideologie'* In the same year, at the height of the protest move-
        ment, the anti-Habermas writing *Die Linke antwortet Jürgen
        Habermas* is published
1969   *Protestbewegung und Hochschulreform*
1970   *Zur Logik der Sozialwissenschaften*
1971   After disputes with the students in the protest movement, Haber-
        mas leaves the University of Frankfurt; he becomes Director of
        the Max Planck Institute for Research into the Circumstances of
        the Scientific- Technical World" in Starnberg; he writes *Theorie
        der Gesellschaft oder Sozialtechnologie* with Niklas Luhmann; in
        the same year he writes *Philosophical - Political Profiles*

1973   Receives Hegel Prize from the city of Stuttgart *Kultur und Kritik* and *Legitimationsprobleme im Spätkapitalismus*
1976   Sigmund Freud Prize of the Darmstadt Academy for Language and Poetry *Zur Rekonstruktion des Historischen Materialismus*
1980   Adorno Prize from the city of Frankfurt; the University of Munich rejects his nomination as honorary professor
1981   Habermas resigns from office as Director of the Max Planck Institute   *Theory of Communicative Action*
1982   Becomes Professor of Sociology and Philosophy in Frankfurt
1983   *Moralbewusstsein und kommunikativen Handelns*
1984   Vorstudien und Ergänzungen zur *Theorie des kommunikativen Handelns*
1985   Receives the Scholl Prize from the city of Munich and the Wilhelm Leuschner Medal from the state of Hesse   *The Philosophical Discourse of Modernity* and *Die neue Unübersichtlichkeit*
1987   *Eine Art Schadensabwicklung*
1988   *Nachmetaphysisches Denken*
1990   *Die nachholende Revolution*

Detlef Horster (b. 1942) is Professor of Philosophy at Hanover University. He is a specialist in the didactics of Philosophy and has published numerous books and articles on the Frankfurt School, neo-marxist theory, epistemology and Socratic thought. He has also written introductions on the work of Ernest Bloch, Alfred Adler, and recently, on Richard Rorty.